YOU WHO MAKE THE SKY BEND

Also by LISA SANDLIN

Stories
In the River Province (2004)
Message to the Nurse of Dreams (1997)
The Famous Thing About Death (1991)

Co-Editor
Times of Sorrow/Times of Grace: Writing by Women of the
    Great Plains/High Plains (2002)

Also by CATHERINE FERGUSON

Retablos
New World Saints (1995)

Chapbooks
The Orchard (2004)
The Sound a Raven Makes (2007)

You Who Make the Sky Bend

Saints as Archetypes of the Human Condition

Lives
by Lisa Sandlin

Retablos
by Catherine Ferguson

Pinyon Publishing
MONTROSE, CO

First Edition: February 2011

Pinyon Publishing
23847 V66 Trail, Montrose, CO 81403
www.pinyon-publishing.com

Library of Congress Control Number: 2010941033
ISBN: 978-0-9821561-8-6

To Susan Ferguson
& Ernestine Sandlin

Contents

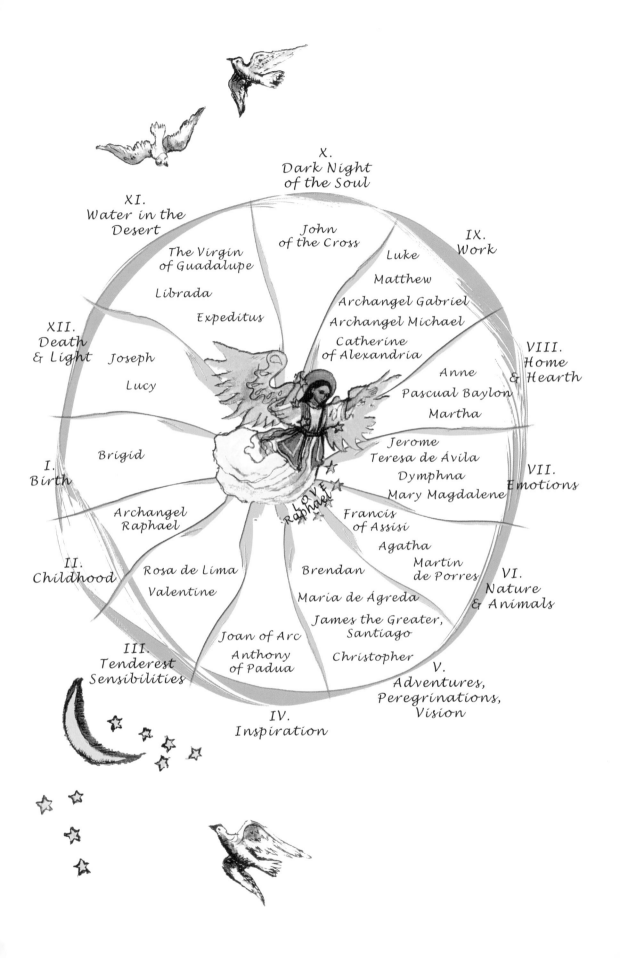

X.
Dark Night
of the Soul

XI.
Water in the
Desert

IX.
Work

John
of the Cross

Luke

The Virgin
of Guadalupe

Matthew

Librada

Archangel Gabriel

Expeditus

Archangel Michael

Catherine
of Alexandria

VIII.
Home
& Hearth

XII.
Death
& Light

Joseph

Anne

Lucy

Pascual Baylon

Martha

Brigid

Jerome
Teresa de Ávila
Dymphna
Mary Magdalene

VII.
Emotions

I.
Birth

Archangel
Raphael

LOVE
Raphael

Francis
of Assisi

Agatha

Rosa de Lima

Brendan

Martin
de Porres

VI.
Nature
& Animals

II.
Childhood

Valentine

Maria de Ágreda

James the Greater,
Santiago

Joan of Arc

Christopher

Anthony
of Padua

V.
Adventures,
Peregrinations,
Vision

III.
Tenderest
Sensibilities

IV.
Inspiration

 Introduction

I was five or six years old when my grandmother's church hosted a preacher who expounded on "Eternity," namely the everlastingness of hell, and to make sure no one considered herself exempt from that location, he stabbed his pointing finger toward the pews. "You!" he hollered. "And you! And *you!*"

I had a few bad deeds on my sheet, so as the preacher intended, my chest flooded with icy waves of guilt and fear. I shuddered them off afterward, but the following afternoon the lingering import of the preacher's sermon knocked me into a trance. I happened to be staring at my grandfather's gun rack, which held a blond-stocked double barrel and two plain rifles, and also, on the slim shelf beneath the guns, a pair of brass knuckles, a Groucho spectacles-set complete with nose and linty mustache, and a tin tube labeled "Peanuts" that when opened shot out a compressed spring covered in snake-printed cloth.

I saw something else. A yellow circle hovered blazing in front of the gun rack. A point of entry did not figure—death thrust you into that circle, and there was no way out of it; it went slickly round and round for all time, for *eternity.*

In short order, I understood four things. I would die. My parents could not shield me because they, being older, would die first. I would die *alone.* And I would be dead forever and ever. The blast of this epiphany scattered the pure azure of childhood. Terror seized me—and bafflement: somehow, understanding these four things, I was supposed carry on as usual, stirring up dirt stews beneath the chinaberry tree, counting my new pencils for school, eating, and sleeping under the attic fan.

However, in a sideways manner, the preacher also confirmed something I had already discovered: I harbored a deep, secret region that, while invisible, was the realest and closest part of my self. I could forget about it most of the day, but not all day, and never at night. I couldn't lie to it because, unlike my head, my soul wouldn't believe me. It *knew.*

In 1974, I met Catherine Ferguson, a young woman with a medieval profession: she painted saints for a living. Catherine had been born in Mexico City, where her artist parents found one another in the studio of Frida Kahlo. As a little girl, she had stared up at one of the most common sights in Mexico, a painting of the Virgin of Guadalupe. The golden fins of light that framed Guadalupe's robed body entranced Catherine. Instead of being terrified, she was inspired. Catherine decided life should be like those fiery rays—illumined, burning.

She was often working on a commission when I visited. Sometimes she was sanding a pre-cut board or applying white gesso to it; then she would set it aside to dry. Sometimes she was painting, hunched over her table with brushes and jars of cloudy water. Her fingers were different colors. I always asked about the personage taking shape on the board beneath her hands.

"Saint," Catherine said, was not the same thing as "perfect." Martha complained when her sister left all the cooking and serving to her. John and James were ambitious and hot-tempered. Jerome, irascible and sarcastic. Asked to keep watch while Jesus prayed in anguish at Gethsemane, the disciples fell asleep.

You Who Make the Sky Bend is a book of retablo paintings by Catherine Ferguson, accompanied by biographies I have compiled from ancient and contemporary sources and poetry. In New Mexican tradition, a retablo is a painting of a saint on wood. These are generally bold-stroked, in primary colors, and they own a quiet integrity. Catherine blends this tradition with Greek iconography and European painting, and her retablos incorporate gold leaf and borders and backgrounds from nature.

Many saint books are organized according to the saints' feast days, the dates of their deaths. This book places them into the wheel of life. It relates each saint to some stage of the human condition, from birth through death and light, inasmuch as saints are associated with a particular occupation or aspect of life; for instance, Anne with the motherhood she desperately wanted.

Excepting archangels and those figures that people created out of their own need, saints were people who began as children, as we all begin. They grew, they lived, they knew the seasons. They had parents, personalities, desires, talents, emotions, and struggles. These human qualities are often what people remember them for, and why we may choose a particular saint as our favorite.

Catherine of Alexandria loved learning. She defied authority, as did Agatha and Lucy. Teresa de Ávila had a sense of humor. Rosa de Lima threw her mother into despair. Martin de Porres' white father abandoned him; Dymphna fled an incestuous father. Brendan loved the sea, and as many of us do, Francis of Assisi talked to animals.

They lived; they also died. But they have not been lost. The saints seem to remain on call, as if their form is a kind of ethereal transmitter tube lit by their filament souls. Many people still talk to them, daily, weekly, or on the unforeseen morning when misfortune pushes past their threshold. And very many people believe they are heard—by the saint, their better selves, their own hearts. Relief floods the gulch the petitioners are huddled in, and more communications are generated, grateful ones made with full breath and voice.

As for the saints whose provenance is doubtful—the ones in this book are Expeditus and Librada—they sprang from such deep human motives that they too took on human appearance and strengths. Procrastinators and those in frantic search of a solution yesterday seized on Expeditus. Women encumbered by brutal husbands or lovers sent prayers to Librada. Needing these saints, people conjured them from relic and desire.

And as for archangels Michael, Gabriel, Raphael—who were never born or died—you have only to consider our culture's fascination with thrilling superheroes to understand their enduring ability to compel allegiance. They dwell with God whenever they aren't dispatched on missions—Gabriel to convey some message, Michael to battle demons, Raphael to protect the innocent. Though they are much above humans in geography, rank, and length of life—forever—even the archangels have human-like parts.

Joshua, Moses' general, looked up and "there stood a man over against him with his sword drawn in his hand." Are you for us or against us? Joshua asked the armed man.

"Nay," said Michael, "as captain of the host of the Lord am I now come."

Daniel, troubled by a mysterious dream, looked up and saw Gabriel "clothed in linen, whose loins were girded with fine gold of Uphaz. His body also was like the beryl, and his face as the appearance of lightning, and his eyes as lamps of fire. ..." Archangel Gabriel is fearsome, and he knows it, for the first thing he says to quivering humans is "Do not be afraid."

Gabriel says it to Daniel, before he interprets the dream, to Zacharias before he tells the old priest that he and his barren old wife will conceive a child. "Fear not," he says to Mary before he announces she will bear God's son. "Fear not," says the angel to the shepherds, who indeed are "sore afraid"—"for behold, I bring you good tidings of great joy."

Gabriel must ease into his annunciations. The humans he awes with his instant, shining appearance perceive that the person standing there is not a person. Unlike them, he cannot be hurt or belittled; he is inviolate. Death itself is his subordinate. Moreover, nothing to Gabriel is a mystery: he *knows*.

As the poet Rilke said: "Every angel is terrifying."

You Who Make the Sky Bend includes thirty-one of the saint images that people have been asking Catherine to paint for close to forty years. On the back of her retablos she writes their stories, as I have done at greater length in the book, stories woven and rewoven from ancient documents, books, legends, human testimonies, and history. The saints attracted me because they had once been flesh and blood people, most of them anyway, and as such, they had to contend with the trials of Earth while constantly aware of eternity. Making butter or boats, cooking, writing, fighting battles and storms and slander, they never mislaid eternity. They spoke of it, they saw it, they heard it.

> Voices, Voices. Listen, my heart, as only
> saints have listened: until the gigantic call lifted them
> off the ground; yet they kept on, impossibly,
> kneeling and didn't notice at all:
> that's how completely they listened.
> —Rainer Maria Rilke, "The Duino Elegies"

Lisa Sandlin
September, 2010

Brigid

(c. 451-525)
February 1

Ireland, Midwives, Babies, Children whose parents aren't married, Blacksmiths, Dairy workers, Fugitives, Chicken farmers, Cattle, Printing presses, Poets

St. Brigid, Goddess of Poetry

Come, be my child:
thee to me I fold.
With my blue veil I cover
and we go on, child and mother.
—Marge Saiser, "St. Brigid Speaks"

Ireland's goddess Brigid, or Bride, was a bringer of life whose feast day celebrated the sun's return, the birth of a new year. Of her, Lady Gregory writes, "Brigid was a woman of poetry and poets worshipped her ... and she was a woman of smith's work, and it was she who first made the whistle for calling to another through the night. And the one side of her face was ugly, but the other side was very comely. And the meaning of her name was Breo-Saighit, a fiery arrow."

The Christian Brigid walks in the goddess's footsteps. She calls words to poets and grants sure-handedness to the crafters of things, acts as balm to the sick and the dying, makes the land bear and flower.

Brigid was said to have been the daughter of Brocessa, a beautiful slave girl, and the nobleman Dubthach, whose jealous wife demanded the slave be sold away to a druid of Connacht. When the nobleman later visited this druid, to ask for a portent for the child his own wife was carrying, he was told, "Happy the child that is born neither in the house nor out of the house." But it was the slave girl Brocessa, fetching a pail of milk warm from the cow, who fell into labor on the threshold, and whose newborn daughter Brigid, delivered neither in nor out of the house, was splashed with the falling milk.

When Brigid grew up, her father Dubthach claimed her from the druid. She milked, tended the sheep and pigs, performed the household tasks. Brigid's face was as lovely as her mother's, but she displeased her father with her endless charity. Whatever was asked of her, she gave.

Dubthach thought to foist her off on the king; he drove to the palace in his chariot and left Brigid to wait outside. A poor man happened by begging, and Brigid, with nothing to hand, gave him her father's battle sword. She answered her livid father that a priceless sword was also suitable as a gift to God. Hastily, the king withdrew from such a purchase. "How can I buy a girl," he demurred, "who holds us so cheap?" Lady Gregory reports a different response. The king said, "I have not the means of purchasing her since she is more precious than silver or gold."

Brigid asked to visit her mother and did so despite her father's refusal. She worked in her frail mother's stead and continued to give to the poor. The druid, hearing of her charity, ordered her to fill a large basket with butter, though he knew she did not have so much. Brigid provided the butter. Amazed, the druid gifted her with twelve cows, but these she did not want. She asked for, and obtained, her mother's freedom.

She longed for her own, as well. And because her vow to God was made and her course deeply felt, she also wished to refuse a suitor who offered her marriage. In response to her prayers, one of Brigid's eyes ulcerated; the man relinquished his claim. Thus she was allowed to become a nun and free. After she had taken the veil, her eye healed, restoring her sight and her beauty.

Brigid founded a monastery and attracted many women who wanted to live freely and to work in her order. She built her cell under a large oak called Kil-dare. A large, industrious community—artisans, carpenters, smiths, cooks, ale and cheese makers, makers of books and bells—sprang up around Kildare's church and around the merry spirit of Brigid herself, for she loved the labors of the country, and it pleased her to welcome guests.

Stories about Brigid link her with light. She and Dara, a blind nun, sat up one night talking of Paradise. They did not notice how the hours had passed until dawn lit the rim of the Wicklow mountains. Sad that Dara could not see how beautiful a day lay before them, Brigid prayed and touched her fingertips to her sister's dark eyes. Dara looked and saw the dewy fields, spring's tender-leafed trees gleaming in the morning, and the far blue arch of the sky. Then she asked Brigid to blind her again, saying that as the world grew dimmer in her eyes, her soul saw God more clearly.

Once Brigid, entering a room, mistook a shaft of sunlight for a wooden beam and draped her damp cloak over it. The cloak hung there until nightfall when one of her sisters reminded her of the patient sunbeam. Brigid then hurried to retrieve her cloak and the ray to catch the sun. A similar tale describes her meeting with St. Brendan. Called to the visitor, Brigid came from tending sheep, tossed her cloak on a sunbeam, and opened her hands in welcome. Brendan had his serving boy drop his cloak alongside, but his twice fell through the clear air. Annoyed, Brendan took the cloak and placed it himself, and this time it hung there, suspended from the light.

Archangel Raphael

September 29

Young people, Lovers, The innocent, Blindness, Healing and healers

San Raphael

"Angel" comes from the Greek word for "messenger," and "Raphael" in Hebrew means "medicine of God." The Book of Tobit, part of the apocrypha, tells the story of Tobit and his son Tobias, who was accompanied on a journey by the archangel Raphael in disguise.

Tobit was an almsgiver and an upright man brought with his kin as captives to Nineveh. Unlike some, he did not take up the customs of that place but "remembered God with all his heart." Nineveh's king Sennacherib executed many people, and though such charity was forbidden, Tobit secretly buried their bodies until at last he was discovered and denounced.

He fled Nineveh, returning after his relatives made his way safe, but when a man of his tribe was killed, Tobit went out into the night and buried him. Troubled, he slept outside by a wall in the courtyard, where sparrows' droppings fell into his eyes, causing white scales to blind him. Tobit despaired for himself and his family and prayed to die.

In a city in Media, a daughter of Raguel named Sara was also praying to die. Her maids blamed her, for she had been bride to a husband seven times, each husband in turn murdered by the devil Asmodeus before the marriages were consummated. If God would not let her die, Sara prayed for His pity.

God sent his angel Raphael as an answer to Tobit and Sara.

Believing he would soon die, Tobit prepared his son Tobias for a journey to Media to retrieve ten silver talents left with kin there. "Deal justly and kindly with all people," he advised his son, "give alms, feed the hungry, remember the commandments, marry a bride from among your own people. If you find yourself poor but love God, Tobias, you are wealthy still."

They searched for someone to accompany him on his journey. Tobias found a man calling himself Azarias who claimed kinship to him, and they set out, Tobias' dog bounding behind them.

In the evening they came to the Tigris River. An enormous fish leapt out of the water. "Catch it," Azarias directed Tobias, "and strip out its heart, liver, and gall." Tobias seized the slippery fish, asking, "What use are those parts?"

"Smoke from the heart and liver will drive away evil spirits," said Azarias, "and the gall is a curing salve for the eyes."

When they came near the city of Rages in Media, Azarias said, "I will speak to the father of Sara, Raguel, so that you should marry his daughter, for she belongs to you." But Tobias knew the story of Sara's husbands and was afraid. If the devil killed him like the others, who would take care of his parents?

Azarias reminded Tobias of his father's wish that he marry a girl of their tribe; as to the marriage chamber, he instructed the young man to take the fish's heart and liver and burn them there, where the devil Asmodeus would smell the smoke and flee.

Sara's father Raguel recognized Tobias as kin and was saddened to hear of his father's blindness. He welcomed the young man as a son-in-law, and the wedding was held, though he feared Asmodeus would strike Tobias the moment the couple were closed into the bridal chamber. A trembling Raguel went out into the night and dug a grave.

Sara and Tobias clutched hands and prayed, their two voices holding off the demon until the young husband could burn the fish's liver and heart just as his companion Azarias had told him. The smoke choked Asmodeus, drove the demon into the deserts of Egypt where Raphael pursued it, struck a deep crevice, thrust the evil thing down into the dark, and sealed the opening with boulders to bind Asmodeus until the last stroke of time.

As the sun rose, maids were sent to the bridal chamber while Raguel and his wife waited in dread. The maids found Tobias and Sara sleeping and rushed to tell the news.

A great feast was laid. Azarias collected the ten silver talents from Tobit's kinsman and brought him back to join the celebration.

Though Raguel pressed Tobias and Sara to stay, Tobias pleaded that he must return, so Raguel gave them his blessing and half of his goods. The couple, with Tobias's dog and Azarias, traveled toward home. On the way Azarias promised that if Tobias treated his father's blind eyes with the gall of the fish, they would open again.

Tobit's wife ran out of the house shouting her son's name. Tobias embraced her and smoothed the gall on his father's white eyes; when Tobit rubbed them, the scales peeled away. Father and son thanked Azarias, Tobias gratefully holding out to his traveling companion half of his father-in-law's gift.

Then Azarias revealed his true name: Raphael, one of seven angels who stand before the Lord and carry to Him the messages of the saints. Frightened, Tobit and his family flung themselves down.

"I have traveled with you all these days, Tobias," the angel said, "though what you saw was a vision. When you buried the dead, Tobit, I was with you, and when you prayed, Sara, I brought your prayers to the Lord. You should not be afraid but give praise."

When they lifted their faces, the angel was gone.

Sara was gathered into the family, and Tobit wrote a joyful prayer to God.

The Gospel of John tells of an angel who stirred the waters of the pool Bethesda. Because the moving water healed the first who stepped into it, this story is associated with Raphael in his guise as guardian of humanity, watching over the wounds of the children of men.

Rosa de Lima

(1586-1617)

August 23

Peru, The Americas, Social services, Florists, Embroiderers, Gardeners, Vanity

St Rosa de Lima

Isabel de Flores was born in Lima, Peru, at a time when Spanish conquest had opened the country to mining and exporting, and Spanish friars and priests just as busily converted the natives and built churches, schools, and hospitals. A servant reported seeing the child's face take the shape of a rose; eventually "Isabel" was set aside, and she was called "Rosa."

Small and delicate, Rosa cultivated flowers in the garden for sale and did fine needlework that provided much of her family's income. But she was like no one in her worldly family.

Taking the penitential Catherine of Siena as her model, she dedicated herself to God with intense fidelity and self-inflicted penances. Young Rosa fasted, wore a hair shirt, scourged herself, slept little—and that on a bed she arranged with broken crockery, tree roots. and a board for a pillow. When her pretty face attracted notice, she rubbed it with pepper, and her slender hands with lime.

To Rosa, her pain was a prayer and an offering. All she said, all she did was prayer. But such behavior maddened her mother María de Flores and caused others to disapprove and gossip about her.

For ten years she refused her parents' wish that she marry, until finally they relented and allowed her to take the habit of St. Dominic. Rosa did not join into that religious community, though; after much argument from her unwilling mother, she retreated into a hut in the garden. There she could be alone to do the embroidery that kept her family and to pray, a slim silver crown with sharp points fixed on her head.

She did not entirely banish the world. Cargoes of gold and silver sailed away to enrich the Spanish nobility while Peruvian natives remained poor and cruelly-worked. Rosa de Lima spoke for them. She nursed sick, outcast women, native and Spanish alike, sometimes begging her outraged mother María to let these women rest in empty rooms of her home.

Always, and alongside her many penances, Rosa experienced grace—a joy that glowed from her, visions, a faithful angel guardian, and visitations of the infant Jesus. De Bussierre tells this story about Rosa de Lima's mornings in her garden hermitage.

> She would call upon all Nature to glorify the Maker of all things with her. Then might the trees be seen bowing over her path, shaking off the dewdrops and rustling their leaves as to send forth harmonious sounds. Then would the flowers sway gracefully on their stalks, half opening their petals to give out their sweetest fragrance, and so in their own way celebrate the praises of God. And with this the birds began to sing their songs and came to perch on Rosa's hands and shoulders, the insects greeted her with their joyful hum—all things, in short, with life or motion joined in concert with the early praises she offered to her Lord.

Rosa increased her fasts and scourgings and suffered fevers and bouts of painful illness. By age twenty-eight, she was so weak that María de Flores dismantled the sharp bed, fearing her daughter's death. Rosa told her it was not time, for since childhood she had held the secret knowledge that she would die on St. Bartholomew's Day, before her thirty-second year.

Perhaps to spare her mother, Rosa left her garden hut to live her last years with the De Massa family, caring for their children, continuing her penances and ecstatic visions. In her thirty-first year, extreme illness and paralysis finished her strength. As St. Bartholomew's Day approached, Rosa revealed that her time was here. Her mother burst into tears, and seeing this, Rosa said aloud: "Lord, I put her into your hands, strengthen and support her, let not her heart be broken."

Midnight tolled. Rosa asked Jesus to be with her and died. Her mother left the bedside where the household was gathered and went into an empty room nearby. María de Flores needed to be alone with the transformation worked by her impossible daughter's prayer: her grief had lifted away, and joy had come full into her heart.

Valentine

(3rd century)
February 14

Love, Lovers, Engaged couples, Happy marriage, Beekeepers, Epilepsy

Several third-century martyrs carried the name of Valentine: a priest of Rome, another in Rome's African territory, and a bishop of Terni. One legend has it that Emperor Claudius, believing that the ranks of his army were thin because men did not want to leave their wives and families, forbade the rite of marriage. Valentine of Rome defied this edict and performed marriages anyway. Claudius, angry at such defiance, had the priest seized.

While jailed, he may have sent a note to the jailer's daughter signed, Your Valentine, but if so, it was the only letter she was to have, for Valentine was beheaded. Both he and the bishop of Terni were buried at the ancient Flaminian Gate, called now the Porta del Popolo or the Gate of the People, but which was in the twelfth century known as the Gate of St. Valentine.

Many scholars believe that St. Valentine's Day was a tendril of Christianity grafted onto the pagan Lupercalia, a fertility festival Romans celebrated on February 15 in honor of the nature god Lupercus, or Pan.

Others hold that St. Valentine's Day was an invention of the fourteenth century. In "The Parliament of Fowls," the English poet Chaucer described February 14th as the day birds gathered to seek out a mate for the coming spring.

> For this was on Saint Valentine's Day
> When every fowl cometh there to choose his mate,
> Of every kind, that men thinketh may;
> And that so huge a noise can they make,
> That earth and sea, and tree, and every lake
> So full was, that hardly was there space
> For me to stand, so full was all the place.

Human lovers as well as feathered ones claimed the day. In 1476, wife-seeker John Paston introduced himself to young Margery Brews: "I beseech you to pardon my boldness and not to disdain but to accept this simple letter to recommend me to you…"

Margery did not disdain; she favored him. A February 1477 letter from her mother invited: "Upon Monday is St. Valentine's Day and every bird chooses himself a mate, and if it like you to come on Thursday night … I trust to God that ye shall speak to my husband and I shall pray that we may bring the matter to a conclusion."

Margery sent her own letter, greeting John as "my rightwell beloved valentine." The problem was her dowry—a meager sum—but John must have visited that Thursday night. The conclusion was marriage. Likely a fond one, as in 1481 Margery Paston chided her husband John for staying overlong in London: "It seems to me a long time since I lay in your arms."

Joan of Arc

(c. 1412-1431)
May 30

France, Soldiers—especially female, Prisoners, Martyrs, Rape victims

When Joan of Arc was born in the village of Domremy, the populace was decimated by plagues and the country split by civil war. The French dukes of Orleans ranged against the French dukes of Burgundy, who had allied themselves with English invaders. No one wore the crown of France. The English claimed it for their boy king Henry VI, since his army held fast the city of Rheims, the place of investiture for all French kings. The Dauphin Charles, the rightful heir, lacked the spine to unseat the English boy. Among themselves the people lamented, "There is great misery in the Kingdom of France."

Joan was a farmer's child. She knew the animals and the art of embroidery and took care with her daily prayers. At thirteen, as she was listening to the Domremy church bells, a brightness lit her family's garden, and a voice sounded in her ear.

Clear among the chimes, the voice said, Do not be afraid. It told her to love God and His house and to be ready to receive guidance from other voices: St. Margaret and Catherine of Alexandria.

On its third visitation, Joan identified the voice as that of the archangel Michael. He gave her a threefold mission: Joan must raise the siege laid to the city of Orleans, see the Dauphin Charles crowned king at Rheims, and liberate France from the clutches of the English.

In 1429 she began, as Michael said she must. She slipped away from her father's farm and persuaded the commander at Vaucouleurs to allow her an escort to Chinon, where the Dauphin held court. Since she traveled with soldiers and lay down beside them to sleep at night, for her own defense she dressed like them.

Joan the Maid left Vaucouleurs on horseback, in soldier's clothing and with her hair cut to her ears. On the journey to Chinon, she exhibited the extraordinary power to inspire which was to be the sum of her short life.

Said one soldier, "I was fired by her sayings and with love for her, divine as I believe." Another said, "On the way we had many anxieties. But Joan repeatedly told us not to be afraid."

At Chinon the Dauphin tested her by hiding himself among courtiers who were dressed in robes richer than his own. But Joan's voices brought her directly to him. She told Charles she was sent by God to help his cause.

"Give me soldiers so that I may take Orleans," she begged. Before committing himself to such a course, the Dauphin ordered her examined by a council of Poitiers clergy. These judged her faith sound and her character good. "Use the aid she offers," they advised.

Not until, the Dauphin's mother insisted, court ladies had verified this strange girl's sex and virginity. It was done, and Joan was pronounced "woman and virgin and maid."

Joan took charge of her army. She permitted no swearing, no camp followers; she had her soldiers confess and hear Mass. But when pressed with chaplets and other objects to bless, Joan laughed to a woman beside her, "Touch them yourself, they will be as good from your touch as from mine."

"This maid," wrote a court councilor, "has a certain elegance. She has a virile bearing, speaks little, shows an admirable prudence in all her words. She has a pretty, woman's voice... She enjoys riding a horse and takes pleasure in fine arms, greatly likes the company of noble fighting men, detests numerous assemblies and meetings, readily sheds copious tears, has a cheerful face; she bears the weight and burden of armor incredibly well."

The maid set out for Orleans in a suit of white armor, followed by her comrades at arms. When she arrived, the renowned captain Dunois refused to send her across the river to fight the English, since the wind was against them and the boats could not move upstream.

Joan rebuked the famous soldier. She spoke as plainly as she was later to speak to the English and to her judges, much to their consternation. For she foresaw, "I shall last a year, hardly longer," and the voice of God was so strong in Joan's ear that all else was faint beside.

No sooner had she spoken than "the wind which was contrary ... changed and became favorable. ... From that moment," Dunois testified, "I had good hope in her."

With good reason. Joan of Arc took the city of Orleans in ten days and drove the English out. She herself laid the ladder to the bastion of the bridge so that the French might storm the city. The Duc d'Alencon, who was to become Joan's friend, reported that "in the matter of war she was very expert, in the management of the lance as in the drawing up of the army in battle order and in preparing the artillery. And at that all marveled."

At Orleans, Joan unmanned the English, earning their hate and derision. Then she and d'Alencon defeated them again at Jargeau and at Patay. The French army was jubilant: the momentum was built to sweep the English from France.

But the Dauphin gave no order. Impatient, Joan appealed to her voices. "And when she heard this voice," Dunois told, "she felt a great joy and desire always to be in that state. And ... she herself exulted in marvelous fashion, raising her eyes to heaven."

Joan roused the Dauphin to action. She and her troops fought through enemy territory to escort him to Rheims, where on July 17, 1429, the Dauphin was crowned Charles VII, King of France.

The archangel Michael had given Joan three tasks. Two were now acquitted. Orleans was taken, the King was crowned, and the soldiers were heard to say, "She will put the King in Paris if it be left to her."

Joan urged the strike for Paris. Characteristically, the new king preferred the whispers of diplomacy to the roar of battle. Excluding Joan from all conferences, he was duped by the English into concluding a brief and foolish truce. He ordered the Maid back to Gien, losing for her her boldly-won military advantage.

Joan finally advanced, but she was wounded in the thigh and had to be dragged from the fray by d'Alencon. The attack failed. Blinking against the light of Joan's large vision, Charles disbanded the army of the coronation and separated her from her comrade d'Alencon.

Joan fought on, unprovisioned and ill-accompanied, though her voices warned her she would be captured. She was, by the Burgundians, on May 23, 1430. Imprisonment was so hateful to her and a life of freedom and movement so dear that twice Joan tried to escape, once jumping from a tower.

The Burgundians sold her to her enemies. While the English could hardly try her for humiliating them in war, they could lock her in fetters and lodge her in a common prison where she was obliged to defend the virginity she cherished. She clung to her soldier's dress. Soon after her nineteenth birthday, Joan of Arc stood trial in Rouen for the crimes of heresy, blasphemy, "vaingloriousness," and the wearing of men's clothing.

Archbishop Peter Cauchon of Beauvais and a tribunal of French clergymen sympathetic to the English interrogated her for five months, and for five months Joan answered them with confounding eloquence and without fear for their power over her. Purity itself, she was tried for impurity. Illiterate, she could not read the charges against her nor the papers she was forced to make her mark upon. A being inseparable from her own conviction, she did not comprehend the cruder human motives that bound her.

The archbishop of Beauvais ordered Joan to recite the Paternoster, and she, in her simplicity, checked him at once. She agreed to do so if he would hear her confession, an act that would have prevented him, as her confessor, from rendering a guilty verdict. Yet as a priest it was his sacred duty to confess all who asked. Beauvais abandoned his request.

Asked about her voice, she faced the archbishop and warned, "The voice told me to answer boldly … you say you are my judge. Consider well what you are about, for in truth I am sent from God, and you are putting yourself in great danger."

Asked if the voice had face and eyes, she responded, "You shall not have that either. Little children say that sometimes men are hanged for having spoken the truth."

Her examiners designed a question to trap her: was she in God's grace? If she answered no, she aligned herself with the devil—if yes, against the church as represented by the churchmen before her. Her response left a ringing silence in the court.

"If I am not," Joan said, "may God bring me to it; if I am, may God keep me in it." Though she loved the church, Joan of Arc chose God over it, and the French above the English. She would deny neither her voices nor her divine purpose.

No one came forward to help her, not the King she crowned or the generals she made victorious or the soldiers whose hearts she had infused with the breath of God. She stood alone, without advocate.

In the very last days of her interrogation, powerfully threatened with the stake, Joan recanted briefly. She signed a paper she could not read. She put on women's clothes.

But when she understood that her home was to be a prison for all her days, she resumed soldier's clothing and recanted her own recanting, "God has sent me by saints Catherine and Margaret great pity for the betrayal to which I consented. … I was damning myself to save my life."

At that reply, a notary recorded *Responsio Mortifera*: Fatal Answer. The archbishop of Beauvais passed outside to the waiting English, saying, "Farewell, it is done."

The town of Rouen watched as Joan of Arc was led to the stake on May 30, 1431. Fervently she called on her saints and forgave those present, asking them—whether they were English or French—to pray for her.

Joan begged a cross made of twigs and urged two priests who stood with her to "hurry, get down" lest they should be burned with her. The fire was lit; along with it doubt and remorse were kindled. Judges and English alike wept at a punishment so cruel for one so brave.

As the flames surrounded her, Joan of Arc turned up her face and cried to Jesus. An English soldier, dragging wood to the pyre of his enemy, was stricken by the cry. Afterward, helped to a tavern to regain his senses, the soldier swore that a white dove had risen above the smoke and flown far up into the curve of the sky.

In 1456, the verdict of the false trial at Rouen was overthrown. A hearing was arranged for any who wished to speak against Joan—none appeared.

One hundred and fifteen witnesses spoke for her. Joan of Arc's confessor Jean Pasquerel recalled, "It was said to her: Never have been seen such things as you have been seen to do. In no book are to be read of deeds like them."

Anthony of Padua

(c. 1195-1231)
June 13

Finding lost things, Good husbands, Health and wealth, Sterility, Fertility, Elderly people, Oppressed people, Poor people, Domestic animals

San Antonio de Padua

On May 30, 1221, the Franciscans held an unusual General Chapter meeting open to all their order, presided over by a vicar general selected by Francis himself. A young Portuguese friar journeyed to observe this meeting. He absorbed the words of every speaker without presuming to offer an opinion of his own. Small, inclined to plumpness, he drew no notice whatsoever. The meeting concluded, and he was assigned as priest to a humble post, a hermitage in Montepaolo, Italy, near Forli.

One day, groups of Franciscan and Dominican friars were sent to Forli for the ceremony of ordination. When the time came for the homily, it was discovered that by an oversight, no one had been chosen to preach. The Dominicans were famous for their preaching; nevertheless, they declined, claiming to be unprepared. The Franciscans shook their heads and said the same.

The flustered superior happened to glance toward the hermitage's young priest, who was called Anthony. Believing this simple rustic barely able to read a missal, the superior saw a way out of his embarrassing predicament: he invited the young man to speak whatever words God would put into his mouth. In this way the necessary homily would be provided; should it be clumsy, no one could be blamed.

All faces turned toward the small priest. Anthony hesitated, but soon his voice warmed and carried to every corner, and he explained the mysteries of divine life and contemplation with such eloquence that the company stood amazed.

Had they known of Anthony's years of study, his performance would not have surprised them.

The priest of the hermitage was born Ferdinand de Bulhoes at Lisbon, Portugal, to wealthy, noble parents. At the age of fifteen, he joined the Canons Regular of St. Augustine, but distracted by jovial visits from friends and relatives, he took himself off to the solitude of a convent in Coimbra. There he stayed and studied for eight years. Intelligent, possessed of a formidable memory, Ferdinand acquired an extraordinary knowledge of scripture and the writings of theologians.

He decided to wear the habit of Francis after being deeply moved by the sight of the first Franciscan martyrs, executed in Morocco, whose bodies were brought to the Church of Santa Croce. Ferdinand took the name Anthony and sailed for Morocco and martyrdom. A severe illness forced him to return. On the way back, his ship, blown by storms, beached on the coast of Sicily. Anthony grew stronger and made his way to the Franciscan meeting where he was appointed to the hermitage near Forli.

Reports of his extemporary speech at Forli reached Francis, who raised Anthony's station to a teacher of theology. But Anthony was to become best known as a preacher and a worker of miracles.

Many of his miracles were recorded, passed down by biographers. A hungry mule, offered both a pail of oats and the Blessed Sacrament, knelt down first to the Sacrament held in Anthony's hand. A young man of Padua named Leonardo confessed that he had kicked his mother; Anthony told him that such a foot deserved to be cut off. The distraught Leonardo ran home and obeyed. Anthony heard of this and hurried to him, laid on his hands and made the leg whole again.

In Rimini, discouraged by the stubbornness of heretics, Anthony went to the banks of the Brenta River and preached to the fishes. According to the *Fioretti*, the fishes lifted their heads from the water to hear. Orderly, their lines ranged before him, the smallest in front, the largest in the deep water; they listened while he spoke as his human audience had not.

> My brothers the fishes, you are bound, as much as is in your power, to return thanks to your Creator, who has given you so noble an element for your dwelling; for you have at your choice both sweet water and salt; you have many places of refuge from the tempest; you have likewise a pure and transparent element for your nourishment. God, your bountiful and kind Creator, when he made you, ordered you to increase and multiply, and gave you his blessing. In the universal deluge, all other creatures perished; you alone did God preserve from all harm.

Even before he had finished, the lines of fishes began to dip their glistening heads, bowing to the truth of his word. Sensibly, the heretics followed the fishes.

Anthony continued to preach, traveling in France and Italy. The papal court in Rome called his preaching "the jewel case of the Bible." At the court's request, he wrote sermons for feast days. In 1231, he returned to the Convent of Padua that he had founded for what was to be his last Lenten season. Thronged by crowds, Anthony spoke against hatred, against enmity, luxury, greed, tyranny. The people of Padua were inspired to reconcile old quarrels, to make restitution to those cheated and harmed; debtors and other prisoners were set free; peace came over their city.

Anthony died near Padua on June 13 of that year. It is said that his death was announced by the church bells ringing of their own accord and children crying in the streets, "The holy father is dead! St. Anthony is dead!"

St. Anthony is much beloved, even today. He is often called on to find lost things, perhaps because of a story popularized in the seventeenth century. A novice borrowed Anthony's psalter without permission—shortly after, a spectre loomed over the young man, and he sprinted to give back the book.

In "The Patron Saint of Lost and Found," poet Greg Kosmicki illustrates this special power of St. Anthony's.

One time in 5th grade I lost my Catechism
so I looked in all the usual places—

under the davenport, under my bed, on the closet floor
stuffed full as usual with all the junk
I cleaned up for the last weeks,
the clothes hamper, the shelf in my room,
under the seats in the cars,
under the kitchen table,
even in my desk.

Nowhere was it to be found.
After a week or so I gave up hope
and started to pray to some Saint
who's the Patron Saint of Lost and Found
or Lost Causes or something like that,
and after a week or so
not really having given up on the Saint
I went and bought another Catechism
because the teacher was bugging me
and I had a lot of stuff to memorize out of it.
The day after I bought the Catechism
like mom made me with my own money
("You won't forget that way, honey.")
I looked down at my feet while waiting
so we could go to school
in the back seat of the station wagon
and saw the missing Catechism.
I couldn't believe my eyes!

I never told anybody about praying
to that Saint
because it was, after all, 1959.

I would have never brought it up even now
if I hadn't been rummaging around
like in an old closet full of toys
through the clutter in my head
where the Saint whose name I have long since lost
stayed, and searched, and found this poem for me.

Brendan

(c. 484-c. 577)
May 16

Sailors, Navigators, Travelers, Older adventurers, Whales

Oh, rough the rude Atlantic, the thunderous, the wide,
Whose kiss is like a soldier's kiss that cannot be denied!
—Emily Lawless, "Fontenoy 1745"

A son of the sea, Brendan was born near Fenit, west of Tralee in County Kerry, Ireland. That night a mist swirled around Fenit, and the child was named for its white rain—*broen finn* or Brendan. Bishop Erc witnessed a flame over the land, and the bishop made St. Ita the child's foster-mother and tutored the boy himself, in time ordaining him a priest. Brendan was to found many monasteries in his long life and to befriend all the apostles of Ireland. His companion in this work was the sea, for he was shipbuilder, navigator, and sailor, and he traveled on the waters, spreading God's houses and His word.

Irish and Latin versions of his life, as well as the widely translated *Navigation of St. Brendan* tell of Brendan's voyages. For these journeys, he built a coracle or small boat like half a shell, covered with hides softened by butter, and added a mast and sail. Later he built a wooden vessel, says the Irish *Life*, "a great marvelous ship and it was distinguished and huge." Having learned of the Land of Promise where God would greet his saints, a heavenly Eden of flowering plants and fruits and stones like gems, Brendan and his monks set out to find it. Their adventures, romantically written by an eighth- or ninth-century ex-patriot Irish monk, enthralled the medieval world.

Brendan and his monks encountered the Paradise of Birds, an island marked by a tree of massive girth. White birds so thoroughly covered its green branches that the tree seemed to sprout white feathers. One bird flew apart, its wingbeats like chimes in the air, and Brendan appealed to it, "Where do so many birds come from? Why are you here?"

The bird spoke, "We share in the fall of Lucifer. Though we did not follow him, neither did we stand with the most faithful. God had mercy on us; we do not suffer. We serve about the earth like other spirits, but on feast days, we claim our tree and sing praises to the Lord, for from here we can see the starry hem of His gown."

Its voice deepening, the bird confided to Brendan that during the years of his voyages, he would spend the holy seasons in four places: the celebration of the Lord's Supper with a provider who would give them much to eat and drink, the Easter vigil on the back of a whale, the Octave of Pentecost here on the Paradise of Birds, and Christmas until the festival of the Blessed Virgin Mary on the island of St. Ailbe.

So it was. Coming Easter and wishing to celebrate the vigil on land, the sailors sought out an island. All disembarked except for Brendan and made a fire on the barren ground to cook. There they stayed the night. But the island swayed with the waves, and in the morning the monks, afraid, ran to their captain, who had them climb aboard the ship again. The island sank and surged through the sea until their fire flickered leagues away. Brendan explained that the island was a fish named Jasconius, the greatest in the ocean, which had provided a resting place for them. Each year during their voyage, they would return to the whale to keep Easter vigil on the rough gray plain of its back.

Fearsome sea monsters sometimes pursued Brendan's ship, and when the navigator called out for help an equally fearsome creature would swim or fly to the rescue and send their pursuer churning below the waves. Even more frightening proved to be the volcanic vision of hell the devil granted Brendan, and the meeting with Judas Iscariot.

In the sea near an island with a black mountain, Iscariot clung to a jagged rock, yoked with a sack suspended by iron prongs. Waves submerged him, filling the cloth sack that beat against his face and head, then receded. Each Sunday for part of the year, this rock was Judas' release from hell until demons came to reclaim him.

Brendan and his crew of monks traveled through gale and calm, keeping the four holy seasons as the white bird had foretold. After seven years on the sea, they sailed through a cloud so dark they lost sight of each other's faces. They passed through this darkness to find themselves on a radiant shore. For forty days, they explored an island pebbled with lovely stones and gems, blazing with the gold trees of autumn, laden with ripe fruits. They could not discover the isle's boundaries, and night never fell. At the bank of a river, a beautiful stranger greeting them each by name forbade them to cross.

"This is the Land of Promise you have sought," the stranger told them. "You have found it only now because God first wished you to know the trials and wonders of the ocean, its storms and its glass, its cities of sea creatures below. When your earthly pilgrimages are done, this land waits for you, full of light."

The *Navigation of St. Brendan* relates many more tales. Father Gearóid Ó Donnchadha instructs us to see it as a "weaving together" of the life of the seafarer and the spirit as lived through the Church's holy seasons. "In particular the story of Judas Iscariot gives us one of the first introductions to the idea of Purgatory, which is very much an Irish innovation."

Though Brendan finished his seven-year voyages, he abandoned neither ship nor sea; he visited Scotland, Wales, Brittany, and founded religious communities. But it was to the green home-ground of Ireland he returned to meet his end. He built an abbey and a school at Clonfert, and there his body lies.

María de Ágreda

(1602-1665)

The Father Custodian of the river province of New Mexico, Fray Alonzo de Benavides, thrilled the Old World with his vivid descriptions of the New. In his *Memorial of 1630,* a combination of travelogue, testimony, and sales tract, he included an account of a woman he had yet to meet.

He related that the Jumanos Indians, having grown fond of a certain priest, used to go and ask for him to come back with them to their lands. The curious Franciscans asked why they came for the priest year after year. The Jumanos pointed to a painting that hung on the wall of the mission.

> They replied that a woman like **that** one whom we had there painted—which was a picture of the Mother Luisa de Carrión—used to preach to each one of them in their own tongue, telling them that they should come to summon the Fathers to instruct and baptize them, and that they should not be slothful about it. And that the woman who preached to them was dressed precisely like her who was painted there; but that the face was not like that one, but that she [their visitant] was young and beautiful. And always whenever Indians came newly from those nations, looking upon the picture and comparing it among themselves, they said that the clothing was the same but the face not, because the woman who preached to them was a young and beautiful girl.

Back in the Jumanos' territory, various Indian captains tired of waiting and ordered the tents struck. But the female visitor spoke to each one of them, telling them that the priests were arriving. They did, three days later. A procession met the soldiers and padres and kissed their crucifixes, Fray Alonso wrote, "as if they were very old Christians." Shown the picture of Mother Luisa, the Indians said that the one who visited them dressed like her but that she was "more handsome and young."

In 1631, Fray Alonso de Benavides sailed back to Spain, where he presented a copy of *Memorial* to the king. Church authorities, having heard of the mysterious visitant in 1623, sent Benavides to interview the abbess of the Convento de la Concepción Purísima in Ágreda.

Sor María de Ágreda was twenty-nine years old, "of beautiful face, of white skin, but of rosy color, and large black eyes." Her interviewer reported that she told him that from 1620 until 1631 she had made regular flights to the territories of New Mexico. Indeed, she had seen Fray Alonso there.

He understood quite well what she meant, that she had bilocated, or been in two places at once: shut in her Spanish convent and simultaneously walking unmapped America. "She convinced me absolutely by describing to me all the things in New Mexico as I have seen them myself," he wrote.

Fray Alonso received from María de Ágreda a letter in her own hand attesting to the truth of her statements. Sor María gave him, he said, "the very habit which she wore when she made those visits"—he described it as gray and white—"and also the veil about which there is a peculiar odor that comforts the soul."

At the time she put habit and veil into Fray Alonso's hands, María Fernandez Coronel y Arana had been abbess of her convent for four years. Except for one three-year interval, she would continue as abbess until her death. She would become known not only for the flights even she called "extraordinary and unusual," but also for the books inspired by her visions.

Sor María held that the last and most famous of these, *The Mystical City of God*, was dictated to her by the Virgin Mary; the book tells of Mary's earthly and heavenly lives and represents her as co-creator of the universe.

At much the same time that Milton imagined the "infernal Serpent" Satan in *Paradise Lost*, María de Ágreda was setting down Mary's valiant battle with Lucifer, who balked at being "ordered to acknowledge as his queen and sovereign, a Virgin, the Mother of Christ, who was to be enriched with such gifts of grace and glory that she would surpass all other creatures, angelic as well as human."

In 1635 and a second time in 1649, the Inquisition summoned Sor María to account for her bilocations. Fray Alonso left behind his glowing letters, but in 1635 he himself took ship for the island of Goa and disappeared.

Sor María defended herself agilely enough. She cited the faults of others, "I find the events in Father Benavides's report all mixed-up," and qualified, "Whether or not I really and truly went in my body is something about which I cannot be certain." The Inquisition retracted its claws, and María de Ágreda died in her convent bed.

But Sor María's destiny is controversy. The Church banned her writings then reversed the ban. She was declared a Venerable centuries ago, but the process of beatification stalled. International groups continue to campaign for her.

She is remembered in the American Southwest as the Lady in Blue.

A 1690 letter from a Fray Damien Manzanet recalls an event that occurred the year before. He had heard of the Lady, and being near to a place she had been seen, Coahuila, he went there himself. The governor of the Tejas tribe asked Fray Damien for a piece of blue baize in which to bury his mother when she died.

On being questioned, the chief explained that his tribe was fond of blue garments, especially for burial, because in years past a beautiful woman wearing blue used to walk down from the hills.

Fray Damien asked how long ago that had been.

He himself had not seen the woman, said the governor, but his elderly mother had, and other people still living, old ones, had seen her.

The editors of the American translation of *The Memorial of 1630* follow this anecdote with a pointed reminder: Benavides stated that María de Ágreda's habit was gray.

However, Benavides's "Letter to the Missionaries," published only in more recent years, contains the description of her order's gray and white habit, and here Fray Alonzo also wrote, "Their cloak is of heavy blue sackcloth."

A legend of the Jumanos Indians claims that when the Lady announced she would visit them no more and walked away into the hills, blue flowers spread over that land.

The Jumanos mostly assimilated into the peoples of the Apaches, but today they are on a mission to revive their tribe. In 2005, a bluebonnet five feet tall was sighted in the Big Bend country of Texas. "When we saw the flower," said tribal historian Enrique Madrid, "we knew the Lady in Blue had come back to help us again."

James the Greater, Santiago

(d. 44)
July 25

Spain, Soldiers, Veterinarians, Hatmakers, Laborers, Pilgrims, Druggists, Equestrians, Horses, Furriers, Tanners, Arthritis and rheumatism

Jesus named his disciples James and John the "sons of thunder," for the two brothers were passionate of temperament, ambitious, and zealous preachers. The historian Bede says of John, "He spoke so loudly that if he thundered but a little more loudly, the whole world would not have been able to contain him."

On one occasion Jesus and his disciples entered a Samaritan village expecting to find food and welcome, but no house would receive them. James and John, incensed, proposed that they bring down a fiery ruin upon these inhospitable people. Jesus dismissed their anger, reminding them that he was come not "to destroy men's lives but to save them."

These followers were his first pupils and, as Jesus wandered and taught, healed and preached, his witnesses. "Freely have ye received," Jesus instructed them, "freely give. What I tell you in darkness, speak in light." After the resurrection, the disciples became apostles who spread across the world, telling what they had seen and learned, and their influence did not end with their deaths on earth.

James is known as "The Greater" in order to distinguish him from a second disciple of the same name, and perhaps because he was larger in stature. Biblical references imply that his mother Salome was the sister of Mary, the mother of Jesus.

In the Gospel of Matthew, Salome requested of Jesus that when he was gone to glory, one brother should sit on his right hand and the other on his left. Jesus warned her that she did not know what she asked. Turning to her sons, he said, "Can you drink of the cup I drink of? And be baptized with the baptism that I am baptized with?"

Rashly they claimed, "We can." The rest of the disciples grumbled among themselves until their teacher explained that his power was unlike that of earthly authorities; that whoever wished to rule should be the servant of all.

But Jesus held these brothers close. They were with him when he raised the little daughter of Jairus from her deathbed and asked them not to tell what they had seen. He asked the same of them when James, John, and Peter accompanied him to the crest of Mount Tabor, where he was transfigured: "and his face did shine as the sun, and his raiment was white as the light."

On the night of their last supper, Jesus went afterward to Gethsemane. The other disciples remained at a distance while he took with him Peter, James, and John. His soul was heavy, he told these three, who were disturbed to see him so sorrowful, and he asked them to stay near him and keep watch.

He knelt down a ways off from them and prayed, "Abba, Father, if thou be willing, remove this cup from me; nevertheless not my will, but thine be done." Luke tells that "being in an agony he prayed more earnestly: and his sweat was as great drops of blood falling down to the ground."

The tired men nearby closed their eyes against their distress and nodded off; they had to be woken with a reprimand. Already Judas Iscariot was striding through the garden, ready to identify Jesus with a kiss.

James must have tempered his fire into the steel of faith, for this apostle preached the word in Judea and Samaria and, tradition has it, in Spain. De Voragine writes of his duels with the magician Hermogenes, whom James converted after he defeated spells of immobility and demons and threw the wily Hermogenes' books of black magic into the sea.

Such a spectacular conversion brought him to the attention of King Herod, and James was the first of the disciples to be martyred, in 44 A.D. The Book of Acts relates that King Herod Agrippa "stretched forth his hands ... and he killed James the brother of John with the sword."

James' power did not die with him. Medieval popes and church historians wrote of occasions when those who invoked his name were saved from danger, slander, and death.

In Spain, James was reborn as Santiago the warrior. Horseback, sword raised, Santiago would gallop out of a cloud to vanquish Spain's enemies. "*Santiago y a ellos!*—Saint James and at them!" became a battle cry heard even in the New World. Even in Africa, the Christian king Nzinga Nkuwu claimed aid from such a vision of St. James in 1506.

Yet it is also in Spain that James lives his longest and gentlest life. Legend has it that his body was sailed in a rudderless boat to Iria Flavia, where a rock molded itself around him, and that this tomb was later rediscovered at Compostela, which became the great site of Christian pilgrimage. Here the son of thunder's sign is the humble cockleshell, called by Sir Walter Raleigh "my scallop-shell of quiet."

Pilgrims wearing his symbol have walked the "Way of St. James" for a thousand years.

Christopher

(late 3rd century)
July 25

Travelers, Transportation, Transport workers, Bachelors, Storms, Bad dreams

If on Christopher thou shouldst gaze
Thou shalt safely wend life's ways.
—Greek Orthodox saying

Christopher was tall and ugly. *The Golden Legend* says that this Canaanite's original name was Reprobus, meaning "outcast," and that he stood twelve feet high. His face was so repulsive to look at that artists have painted him with the head of a dog. But his legend has remained compelling even after the Roman Catholic Church scratched Christopher from its list of saints.

This hideous giant wanted to serve the greatest prince in the world. Accordingly, he offered his service to a king, who instantly accepted him. However, one day a court jester pranced around the throne, singing a song that mentioned the devil. The king made the sign of the cross, and Christopher asked him why. The king told him he did so to ward off the power of this evil being.

"Then he must be stronger than you," said Christopher, "and since I want to serve the most powerful, I will go and find him."

Christopher was trekking across a desert when he met a legion of soldiers. The most vicious of these asked him where he was bound. To find the devil and serve him, Christopher said.

"You have found him," whispered the malignant soldier. Christopher fell into step with them, marching alongside his new master.

They came to a road, and to one side of it stood a wooden cross. The devil flinched and detoured his dark troops away from the cross into a wasteland before veering back to the road. "Why did you lead us away?" Christopher asked, but the devil's mouth stayed shut. "Tell me," the giant demanded, "or I will leave you at once." Shuddering, the devil told him of a fearsome man named Christ who had been nailed to such a cross.

"Since he makes you tremble, you cannot be the prince of the world, and I will go and find the one who is." Christopher deserted the devil to search out a greater master.

No one could direct him until he met a hermit who tried to teach him the ways of Christ. "If you want to serve him," said the hermit, "you must make a habit of fasting."

Christopher, scanning the vast length of his body, answered that he could not fast. What else could he do?

"Pray to him," the hermit said.

"I don't know how to pray. Is there another kind of service I can do?"

The hermit asked him if he knew of a certain treacherous river. When Christopher nodded yes, the man said he was surely big enough to ferry people over this river, and perhaps that was a service that would take him to Christ.

"That service I can do," agreed the giant. Christopher journeyed to the river, built himself a hut beside it, cut a staff to balance him in his work, and offered his broad back and tremendous strength to any travelers who wished to ford the river.

One day a child called to him. Christopher lofted the little boy onto his back, took his staff, and waded into the river. He was baffled when the child's small body began to bow his shoulders down. Stride by stride, the child's weight increased, and the river turned wild. Christopher fought through roiling, bursting, foaming waves, bending lower and lower under the child's staggering weight until he thought he would sink, and they would both be swept away.

At last he stumbled out of the torrent and set the child down on the far bank. "My boy," he sighed, "you felt so heavy I might have been holding the whole world on my back."

"So you were," answered the boy. "You were carrying the one who carries the whole world. Put that staff in the ground beside your hut if you need proof." Then the child was gone.

Christopher splashed back across the river. He planted the pole, saw it sprout branches and green leaves and fruit and knew then he had found the one he wanted to serve. Through trials and persecution, the massive man with the ugly face served that prince, and he died for him.

Francis of Assisi

(1181 or 1182-1226)
October 4

Animals, Ecology and ecologists, Environment, Peace, Dying alone,
Merchants and tapestry workers, Zoos

ST. FRANCIS TALKING TO THE BIRDS

> Everything is a miracle. What is the water we drink, the earth
> we tread, the night which descends upon us each evening
> with its stars; what are the sun, the moon? Miracles, all of
> them. Just look at the humblest leaf of a tree, just look at it in
> the light—what a miracle! The Crucifixion is painted on one
> side; you turn the leaf over on the other and what do you see:
> the Resurrection! It is not a leaf, my brothers, it is our hearts!
> —Nikos Kazantzakis, "Saint Francis"

Francis was a rich man's son who paid little attention to his education, preferring to spend his father's money on fine clothes and carousing. A singer, a wit, happy and especially generous, Francis was well-liked and indulged in every quarter.

Illness and a dream interrupted his revels. Francis dreamed of a hall that held many pieces of armor, all signed with the cross. He woke and determined to join a military adventure, jubilantly believing he would be a great prince. Instead, he found himself drawn to things of the spirit. Meeting a ragged man on the road, Francis gave him the dashing outfit he wore. He turned away from raucous nights, telling his bewildered friends that he was "about to take a wife of surpassing fairness." By this he meant Lady Poverty—a way of life he had to search out, to stumble toward, for he did not find her at once.

He was praying at a toppled old chapel called St. Damian's when a voice said to him, "Go, Francis, and repair my house, which you see is falling into ruin." Francis hurried to his father's cloth shop, piled up lengths of linens and wools, and galloped off to a market where he sold the horse as well as the goods. He returned to thrust the money at the priest of St. Damian's, but the priest, wary of Francis' father, Pietro Bernardone, would not touch it. Francis flung it down on a windowsill.

While his enraged father searched for both son and money, Francis hid in a pit near St. Damian's for a month. He emerged disheveled and walked toward Assisi, jeered at and pelted with mud by townspeople who knew him as a pampered favorite.

His father heard the clamor and ran out. He took hold of his son, chained him in the basement, and rode off to retrieve the money Francis had abandoned at the old chapel. Francis' mother unlocked his chains, but when Pietro strode into the house, the gold clinking in his pocket, he dragged his son before the bishop to disown him. Francis did not protest.

Saying that the clothes he had on were also his father's, Francis stripped off the pretty garments, and naked, gave them back. The bishop of Assisi perceived a mysterious spirit in the young man before him. He draped Francis with his mantle and became his helper.

Now Francis went about in laborer's dress he marked with a cross in chalk, singing praises to the Lord. Robbers beat him and left him in a ditch full of snow. Francis climbed out and went off singing again. Cheerful and courteous, he begged alms for sustenance, fetched and scrubbed in a monastery kitchen, befriended lepers, aided the poor and visited the hospitals.

Once, however, he rebuffed a man who asked him for alms. Afterward his heart suffered so much that he fervently arranged it in a new way: he pledged himself never to turn away anyone.

Francis went back to the old chapel of St. Damian's and built it up again from its foundation. Carrying stones for the masons, he next helped repair an old church dedicated to St. Peter, and then an abandoned little chapel called Portiuncula, two miles from Assisi.

He made himself a hut at that place, and in 1209 at the feast of St. Matthew, became drunk on that Gospel's words: "Freely have you received, freely give." Francis gave away everything he owned and wore only a thin tunic he tied with rough cord. At last, Lady Poverty stood before the cloth merchant's son with her arms open.

Townspeople, even the mud-pelters, began to consider Francis worthy of respect. Some rich and well-known men joined the Poverello, or Little Poor Man, and took up his way of life, as did a wealthy young woman, Clare, who formed a like group of women. Francis wrote rules for his band and carried them to Rome for approval in 1210. Pope Innocent III, after a dream in which he saw Francis hold up a wall of a tottering church, authorized his preaching.

As Francis preached, so he lived, and as he lived, so he prayed.

Lord, make me an instrument of your peace.
Where there is hatred, let me sow love;
Where there is injury, pardon;
Where there is doubt, faith;
Where there is despair, hope;
Where there is darkness, light;
Where there is sadness, joy.
O Divine Master, grant that I may not seek so much
To be consoled as to console;
To be understood, as to understand;
To be loved, as to love.
For it is in giving that we receive;
It is in pardoning that we are pardoned;
It is in dying that we are born to eternal life.

In the next fifteen years, Francis labored mightily with his order of Friars Minor, which spread to Umbria, Tuscany, Lombardy, and Ancona. He rewrote their rule and held chapter meetings that gathered all Franciscans.

In 1219, he traveled to Damietta, burning to convert the Saracens; his interviews with sultan Malek al-Kamil were polite but fruitless. Then his closest followers called him back to Italy. Francis was disturbed by dissension among his brothers and by the rich convent in Bologna where they met. He refused to stay in such a house, moved to a simpler dwelling, and summoned his brothers to him.

Again he rewrote the rule, never relaxing the poverty, humility, and freedom to preach that were its basis. All this time, he practiced the strictest poverty himself and taught by example simplicity, kinship, love and compassion for all things.

Once his brothers watched him cradle a rabbit that then repeatedly jumped up and nestled back onto his lap after he had set her down. On another occasion, seeing a flock of birds—doves, crows, and daws—in the roadside trees, Francis ran to greet them, calling, "My brothers, birds!"

The birds did not fly away but stayed to listen as the worn, bearded man with the clear voice praised their feathers and their home the air and told them to love their creator always. He touched their heads and blessed them. Francis spoke to animals of all kinds—and to flowers, gardens, vineyards, and stones—naming them his brothers and sisters.

In 1224, the exhausted Francis retreated for a time to Mount Alvernia, where the marks of the stigmata appeared on his body. He let his sleeves fall over his hands and put on shoes and stockings to prevent the world from seeing these signs of favor.

His strength and eyesight were failing. He paid his last visit to Sister Clare at St. Damian's, and there, in spite of wretched pain, Francis poured out an exuberant joy in "The Canticle of the Sun," and made a tune for it, which he taught the company to sing. He praised "Brother Sun, beautiful and radiant in all his splendor; Sister Moon and the stars, precious and beautiful; Brothers Wind and Air; Sister Water; cheerful and powerful Brother Fire, strong Mother Earth who feeds and rules us, and Sister Death, whose embrace none of us escapes."

Francis' health slipped further; blindness crept in on him. Cardinal Ugolino made him submit to an excruciating and useless operation on his eyes; doctors applied their potions to no effect.

Francis asked to be taken back to Portiuncula, the first home he shared with Lady Poverty. Near Assisi, he had the stretcher-bearers set him down. He could not see, but he turned toward the town and blessed it and his brothers before he was carried on to welcome Sister Death.

Agatha

(d. 251 or 253)
February 5

Nurses, Breast cancer, Fire, Earthquakes, Sterility

Agatha's story is like that of Lucy and Catherine of Alexandria, telling of a beautiful and wealthy Christian girl persecuted by a pagan official. The man Agatha defied was a Sicilian magistrate in Catania named Quintianus. Like other persecutors, he craved to see the girl humbled so that he might wallow in his own power. But the girl's faith held her safe during her trials, even in a brothel whose tapestries and gilded trinkets could not disguise its imitation of joy.

Agatha withstood the efforts of Aphrodisia, the procuress, to change her into a prostitute. "Aphrodisia's promises are as raindrops," Agatha said, "and her threats as rivers, and however hard they beat upon the foundation of my house it cannot fall." The procuress dragged her back to the magistrate, grumbling that one could more easily split rocks than turn this girl from her love of Christ.

Quintianus sentenced Agatha to jail. She went willingly. She went as willingly to the rack. A maddened Quintianus then commanded his executioners to cut off Agatha's breasts, and still the girl mocked her tormentor, declaring that he could not touch her spirit. Mortified at losing face before his people, the magistrate ordered his servants to hurl her into a prison cell and to bring her no food, no doctor to tend her wounds, not even a cup of water.

Of another martyr who suffered Agatha's mutilation, Spanish poet Federico Garcia Lorca wrote:

> Through the red holes
> where once were her breasts,
> tiny skies are now seen
> and rivulets of white milk,
> a thousand little trees of blood
> cover all her back

In the night an old man bearing a bundle of salves and herbs entered her cell. A light surrounding his white hair illuminated the cell's rough-cut stones, the bloody girl, the jailers cringing at the door. Agatha thanked him for his good intentions but told him the Lord could cure her with a single word. The old man smiled, saying that he was the Lord's apostle Peter, and that she was indeed healed. Agatha knelt on the stone floor and, lifting her arms to the light, found her wounds vanished and her body restored. The keepers fled without locking the door, but she did not run away, for Agatha knew what they did not, that she was always free, always whole—and she refused to let her jailers be blamed for her escape or to lose the patience that promised her heaven.

Quintianus revealed his smallness by demanding more torture: Roll her naked across potsherds and live coals! But as this ugly punishment was carried out, an earthquake also rolled; the quake cracked the columns of his house and toppled his pagan statues from their marble pedestals. The people of Catania burst in, crying that his cruelty to Agatha had brought this disaster down on them. Quintianus again locked the girl in prison, and there Agatha asked the Lord in His mercy to take her spirit.

The beleaguered magistrate galloped away in his chariot, but after a short distance, his two horses snorted a fiery breath, reared, and threw him into a river to drown. One year later, the great volcano Etna exploded in flame; boulders and lava spewed toward the town of Catania. People who had not believed before ran to Agatha's burial place. They seized the veil that hung over her tomb and unfurled it into the path of the burning stream, which halted at that spot. They were saved, and with them, their children, their houses and fields—all remained untouched and whole.

Some people in the Pyrenees called Saint Agatha *Santo Gato*, Saint Cat, and held that she punished women who worked on her day. One story tells of a housewife who was that very day baking bread. A cat sidled into her house, sprang up, and swiped a bit of dough. When the housewife cried "Get out!," the creature turned its yellow eyes on her and said, "I am not a cat. I am Saint Agatha. Look up." And the woman looked up to see flames licking the beams of her house.

Martin de Porres

(1579-1639)
November 3

Peru, Nurses, Health care workers, Mixed-race people, African Americans, Barbers,
Social justice, Public health, Race relations, The poor

His baptismal entry read, "On Wednesday, the ninth of November, I baptized Martin, son of an unknown father."

He was born in Lima, Peru, the natural son of a Spanish grandee and Ana Velasquez, a black woman of Panama. The mixed-race boy did not receive the protection of his father, who deserted the family after a daughter was born. Juan de Porres did acknowledge his dark-skinned child—as well he might, for in books the father's name lingers in a few lines only because of the son's. Martin de Porres is the first black saint of the Americas.

In later years he would fast and flog himself; even as a child, he prayed long hours. Charity sprang from his small hands—like Ireland's Brigid, Peru's Martin gave away anything asked of him, indeed anything in reach, sometimes a difficulty to his struggling mother. Ana Velasquez, herself an herbalist, apprenticed her twelve-year-old son to a barber/surgeon. Martin learned to dispense potions and elixirs, to set bones, let blood, bind up wounds.

The trade pleased Martin; he was a healer by nature. Soon he outstripped his master. Martin's "semblance was happy and peaceful," and many a groaning patient called for the apprentice's comfort at their bedsides, for Martin's soul shined in his smile, and it was an extraordinary soul.

At sixteen, he went to the Dominican friars of the Convento del Santo Rosario as a *donado*, performing the menial tasks of sweeping and cleaning toilets, and there he remained, happy and useful, for nine years. His indignant father, then governing Panama, tried to have his son fully accepted into the Order, only to find that despite laws that prohibited races of color from being full lay brothers, the Dominicans had already invited Martin among them on several occasions. Martin had turned them down.

He joined at the age of twenty-four, as a regular lay brother, and took over the infirmary. Martin de Porres became a familiar figure, armed with his brazier and branch of rosemary to perfume fetid sick rooms, his bundles of bandages, and his beautiful presence. He was known to appear at a bedside, though the door was locked, bringing a patient whatever he or she most desired: a cool cup of water, a fruit out of season.

Martin doctored African slaves shipped to Peru as laborers, and he was said to be a friend to Rosa de Lima, who also cared for the outcast and prayed for them from her garden hermitage. His love extended to all creatures, for he spoke to and was heeded by animals, always seeing to their welfare.

In time Brother Martin established an orphanage and a foundling hospital. He proved to be expert at collecting funds for the order and for his limitless charities. Such was his reputation that the rich and the noble opened their purses wide when Martin de Porres stood smiling at their handsome doors.

When he died he was already perceived as a saint by the people of Lima. Twenty-five years later, the body of the black Dominican brother was exhumed, discreetly, yet Lima poured in: viceroy and lords, the entire city government, priests from different orders, "captains of the Infantry, and many gentlemen, and other honorable persons of this Republic."

All these lofty personages, as well as the poor of Lima, knew the stories about Martin de Porres. He levitated as he prayed and a light glimmered from him; without leaving his convent, he appeared in a far country to nurse a sick friend; he cured impossible cases. And they would have been able to recite how, on a certain occasion—and on another and another—he acted with humility and kindness. The stories are very many, and they are still told.

Once the wardrobe containing priests' clothing was overrun by mice that chewed holes in the vestments. Martin reprimanded the creatures and promised that if they would take up a new home in the garden he would feed them. There was a scuffling. Alert eyes appeared from every drawer. Mice dove from the wardrobe and swarmed out to the spot Brother Martin had set aside for them. From that day, he brought them scraps from the infirmary, and the garments in the wardrobe did not have to be mended.

One day Martin was talking with an elderly brother, a good but stern old man. A young priest walked by wearing a fancy pair of shoes. The scandalized old priest exclaimed, "What do you say about the light-mindedness of that young brother?"

Martin believed that God permitted this minor vanity in order to win sinners back to Him.

"Some people," he said, "are so used to fine things that even a mention of austerity scares them. If a person like that were to come here, do you think that your severe appearance and those shoes as big as boats that you are wearing would inspire trust in his heart? Not at all! But if he saw that young priest with his beautiful little shoes, he might think 'Now there is one who will understand me!' And he would go to confession, and then the grace of God would do the rest."

Martin de Porres smiled, then he laughed, and the old priest laughed with him. How could he resist?

Jerome

(c. 347-420)
September 30

Scholars, Librarians and libraries, Schoolchildren, Archivists, Translators,
Archeologists, Temper

Late in Jerome's life, a lion holding up one huge paw is said to have appeared at the gates of his monastery. The frightened monks scattered. Only Jerome, old and weak, did not fear the wild beast.

He pulled himself upright by the aid of a rope fixed above his narrow bed and came forward to welcome the lion as a fellow creature. Jerome took the paw the lion lifted toward him and discovered embedded in the sore flesh a huge thorn. He called his brothers from their hiding places to wash and treat the wound.

As the lion healed, the monks reported a remarkable change: its savage nature became so companionable that the beast often lay at Jerome's feet. The monks claimed they trusted it to guard the donkey that each day carried their bundle of firewood from the forest. The lion, a fearsome prospect on its arrival at the gates, proved a useful servant.

Jerome, ascetic, linguist, translator, Christianity's brilliant scholar, was known equally well—and disliked—for his sarcastic temper. His quarrelsome reputation is as enduring as his mighty work. Ten centuries after Jerome's death, Pope Sixtus V, on studying a painting of Jerome penitently beating his breast with a stone, commented dryly, "You do well to use that stone; without it you would never have been numbered among the saints."

Born Eusebius Hieronymus Sophronius in 342 in northern Italy, Jerome was sent early to Rome. There under the pagan tutor Donatus, he mastered Greek and Latin and was influenced by the best writers in those languages.

Traveling to Antioch some time later, Jerome had a dream in which Christ chastised him for valuing the pagan wisdom of Cicero, "for where thy treasure is, there is thy heart also." Jerome, stricken, made this distinction: "Plato located the soul of man in the head; Christ located it in the heart." He returned to Rome to be ordained. Although he wished to spend his life as a recluse, he was forced from the city when clerics he had denounced for their debauched lives concocted a plot to drive him away.

Jerome settled in Chalcis, a wilderness near Antioch. He lived as a hermit and continued his studies even while suffering visions of temptation. "My face grew pale with hunger," he wrote, "yet in my cold body the passions of my inner being continued to glow."

To subdue the "ardent heat" of his nature, Jerome read theology and Greek texts, and he learned Hebrew. "I put myself in the hands of one of the brethren who had been a Hebrew before his conversion, and asked him to teach me. … What efforts I spent on that task, what difficulties I had to face, how often I despaired, how often I gave up and then in my eagerness to learn began again."

When he returned to Rome, the learned hermit was chosen as secretary to Pope Damasus I. Jerome was given the great work that he would complete long years later in Jerusalem. He revised and retranslated The Gospels, The Psalms, and other New Testament books from Old Latin. He formed the church liturgy into a beautiful and orderly cycle, confirmed as standard for the entire Catholic Church.

During this time he also became spiritual advisor to a group of Roman noblewomen, including the wealthy Paula. Slanders arose over their friendship, even though Jerome instructed the women according to his own ascetic ways, saying, "Let your companions be women pale and thin with fasting."

Critics questioned such unnatural renunciation: why should fasting be more holy than enjoying the food God provides, virginity a state superior to marriage? Jerome turned his scathing tongue on those he believed to be in error, earning himself many enemies.

Of one Onasus, "a windbag," he wrote, "Let your nose not be seen upon your face, and let your tongue never be heard in conversation. Then you may possibly be thought both good-looking and eloquent."

Jerome retreated to Antioch, then to Jerusalem where his home became a stone cell near the birthplace of Jesus. He founded a school and a hospice, and by such devotion attracted disciples. He fasted, prayed, and worked.

Even during his years of labor on the scriptures, Jerome opposed any scriptural doctrine he considered harmful to the church. "I fear all that is too safe," he said. At the cost of old friendships, he refuted the writings of Helvetius, Jovinian, and Origen, whose learning he nevertheless admired, and plunged into a dispute with Augustine, who revered him.

With like force, Jerome persevered in his translation of the Old Testament from Hebrew into Latin. "He rests neither by day nor night," a contemporary said. "He is always either reading or writing."

At last he finished. He sent his work to Rome, where his version of the Old Testament was deemed official by church fathers.

In 1455, more than a thousand years after Jerome laid down his weary pen, the first Bible was printed in Germany. The text used was Jerome's.

Teresa de Ávila

(1515-1582)
October 15

Spain, Religious workers, The sick, Headaches, Bodily ills, The death of parents

THERESIA

Nada te turbe	Let nothing disturb you
Nada te espanta	Let nothing frighten you
Todo se pasa	Everything passes
Dios no se muda	God never changes
La paciencia	Patience
Todo lo alianza	Obtains everything
Quien a Dios tiene	Whoever has God
Nada le falta	Lacks nothing
Solo Dios basta	God alone is enough
—Teresa de Ávila	

In the Spain of Teresa's time, a churchman at your door thundering, "In the name of the Holy Inquisition" meant to be deserted by father and friends, by the mother who bore you. That religious tribunal ruled the country by fear and fire. Friends once cautioned that Teresa's activities had stirred up so much gossip that they were afraid the Inquisition would turn its slitted eyes toward her. Teresa's reaction: "They only amused me and made me laugh for I never had any fear about this."

Around the time she began to reform the Carmelites, a priest in the pulpit pointedly denounced nuns founding new orders. The nun sitting by Teresa, alarmed, glanced over at her sister and saw that *"con gran paz se estaba riendo"*: she was quietly laughing to herself.

She did complain to Jesus about all the gossip. She heard this response: "Teresa, that is how I treat all my friends"—and retorted, "No wonder you have so few."

"God, deliver me from sullen saints," Teresa de Ávila once said. She was no pale, fasting maiden. She meant to be good, and she meant to know God. She was, and she did, without grimness or flagellation. Of her custom of never speaking ill of others, she wrote wryly, "It came to be realized that in my presence people could turn their backs to me and yet be quite safe."

Teresa Sanchez de Cepeda y Ahumada, granddaughter of a Jew forced to convert to Christianity, daughter of strict, loving parents, sister of conquistadors, was born near Ávila. She was a contemporary of Cervantes and Shakespeare. She too wrote prose—and poems:

> If You want me to rest
> I desire it for love;
> If to labor
> I will die working

She didn't write for secular publishers or for the theatre, but at the behest of her confessors. She wrote at top speed, and the passionate sincerity of her voice still leaps from the page.

Like Martin Luther she accomplished reform, though not through dramatic public displays. Teresa was a woman of vast charm and equally vast will, her frailty countered by hard work, boldness, and earthy humor. She was an expert diplomat; stealthy, some might say, and her many friends, including the King of Spain, could be counted on to come down on her side. At the same time, she possessed a mystical nature whose communion with God grew slowly more ecstatic and more still.

At the age of seven, Teresa and her older brother Rodrigo ran away, resolved to be martyrs; once their heads were cut off by the Moors, they would fly straight to heaven. An uncle foiled their plans and returned the two to their worried mother. Next they decided to be hermits; to construct their hermitage, they piled up stones, which kept falling down.

Teresa became a flirtatious girl who cared about her looks and liked perfumes and her frivolous cousins. She was only thirteen when her mother died. Bereft, she flung herself before an image of Mary and begged the Queen of Heaven to be her mother. Her concerned father sent her to a convent to be educated by Augustinian nuns, but Teresa fell ill there. Her father brought her back home and would not hear of her returning to convent life.

She went secretly to the Carmelite convent in 1536 when she was twenty. Once the deed was done, her father agreed. There followed eighteen years of religious life during which Teresa struggled to grow into her true self.

The convents then were comfortably social houses free from responsibility and poverty. Nuns chatted with visitors in the parlor; they came and went. Through an uncle Teresa had learned about "mental prayer" and tried it but soon neglected the practice. She pleased people; she spent time in petty employments. "I delighted in being thought well of," she said, "I was particular about everything I did and all this I thought was a virtue."

At the age of twenty-three she suffered a serious illness. Her father took her for treatment; however, Teresa worsened so much that a grave was dug for her. The effects of this illness were paralysis and weakness that lasted three years and recurring bad health throughout her life.

It was not until after her father died—she said, "It seemed my soul was being wrenched from me, for I loved him dearly"—that Teresa came back to mental prayer: "I began to return to it … and I never again abandoned it."

This was not the prayer recited aloud with others; rather, it was a silent refuge inside the self where alone she listened to God. "The words are not heard with the bodily ear," Teresa wrote, "yet they are understood much more clearly … it is impossible to fail to hear them. …When God talks in this way to the soul … I have to listen, whether I like it or no." She described mental prayer as "an intimate sharing between friends; it means taking time frequently to be alone with Him who we know loves us."

In 1558, Teresa began to experience visions and raptures. She had her most extraordinary experience in 1559, what has come to be called the

"Transverberation," when a small angel holding a large golden dart tipped with fire plunged it, she wrote, "several times into my heart … when he drew it out, I thought he was carrying off with him the deepest part of me; and he left me all on fire with great love of God." These supernatural events, these favors, troubled her, and she consulted many confessors, some of whom, as young as she, suggested the devil was deceiving her.

Finally she encountered mentors who recognized her unique gifts. Encouraged at last, Teresa determined to found the Discalced Carmelite nuns, which would return to this branch of the Carmelite order the essential rules of poverty, enclosure, and prayer. She met with resistance. Her immediate superiors were "astonished that a little woman should found a convent against their will." Teresa went over their heads to the bishop. She persevered and founded the St. Joseph Convent in 1561. Opposition broke out against her.

Once started, however, she was a force and rarely enclosed. Though in 1562 she was ordered to retreat to St. Joseph's and keep herself there—"the most peaceful years of my life," she later commented—Teresa spent most of the next twenty years traveling Spain's roads in all weathers. Episodes of illness recurred. She went on; she selected novices, insisting they be intelligent, secured houses for her nuns, moved them in, and made sure a capable prioress was in place. Teresa hired workmen for repairs, handled accounts and correspondence, quarrels and dissension, and a hundred other matters.

Amongst these endless tasks, she devoted two hours of every day to intense contemplation and, instructed to do so by confessors, she wrote her great books on the nature of the soul's progress in prayer.

She established seventeen convents in twenty years. She also founded houses for men with the help of young John of the Cross, a mystic like herself. Teresa left Burgos, her last foundation, in 1582, very sick, longing to go home to Ávila.

She was sixty-seven years old in a time when a common lifespan was thirty. She was the most famous nun in Spain, worn from her exertions. Nonetheless, a stripling priest brought orders from a superior that Teresa was to oversee the election of a prioress in Alba de Tormes and to attend a pregnant duchess there.

She obeyed but collapsed on the road. Unsurprisingly, both commissions were fulfilled. The duchess managed to produce the baby by herself. Teresa duly oversaw the election, then died in the arms of the nun who traveled with her.

"It pleased the Lord," Teresa de Ávila wrote in her autobiography, "that in my earliest years I should receive a lasting impression of the way of truth." That impression was brought about by words she and big brother Rodrigo repeated as boisterous children. *"Para siempre—siempre!"* they chanted. *"Para siempre—siempre!"*

"For—ever—ever. For—ever—ever."

Dymphna

(7th century)
May 15

Therapists, Caregivers, Mental and nervous disorders, Victims of violent crime

Legend has it that Dympha was the daughter of Damon, a pagan Irish king, and a Christian mother of uncommon grace. When Dymphna had grown almost to womanhood, her mother died, and her father raged and wept. He set off on a mad journey through the western world in search of a woman as lovely as his wife, that he might marry again. But the king could not find one like her, whose braided hair called the sunlight, whose sea-green eyes gentled his growling spirit. He trudged towards home, each step a misery, for grief and desire weighted the hem of his cloak like rough stones.

Dymphna rushed to welcome her father. The joy in her face transfixed the tired king: his wife seemed returned to him in all her beauty. If only Dymphna were not his trusting child. If only he were not father and protector, all the years of his given life.

But your burdens are so very great, whispered his secret voice.

Link by link, the voice began to forge an evil chain around his soul: What is a mere blood covenant to a king? Love is love, a husband protects. This fair girl stands within the reach of your arm.

The chain was complete; Damon embraced his daughter, saying they would marry, and clasping her unwilling hand, pulled the girl toward his bed.

Dymphna broke away. She fled her father's house along with her confessor, an elderly priest named Gerebernus, and the two took sanctuary near Antwerp, Belgium, in the town of Gheel.

Damon and a troop pursued, crossing borders into Belgium. There an innkeeper, examining the king's coins, pronounced them useless, for they were a difficult currency to exchange. This remark told Damon that the man must have handled like coins recently, and he knew that his daughter lodged nearby. His soldiers routed the runaways in Gheel, where by the king's order, they beheaded old Gerebernus.

Again Damon caught hold of Dymphna, but she was not the same girl who once ran joyously to greet him. Her gaze was bitter as a winter midnight, her heart barred like an iron door.

"Never, my father," said Dymphna, "never."

The king's sword flashed, and the head of his brave daughter came to rest at his feet.

St. Dymphna is invoked against insanity and nervous illnesses, and many accounts of cures and miracles cite her presence. Two ancient sarcophagi, in one a brick carved with the name *Dymphna*, were discovered at Gheel. Reversing the legend, painters have shown a girl with sword in hand and at her feet, a devil bound in chains.

Mary Magdalene

(1st century)
July 22

Women, Contemplatives, Hairdressers, Perfumers, Pharmacists, Glovemakers, Sinners,
Sexual temptation

Mary Magdalene / Troparion

Lord, this woman who fell into many sins
Perceives the God in you,
leads the woman who come with grief
and myrrh to your grave
Alas, what a desperate night I've traveled through:
extravagant the desire, dark and moonless
the needs of a passionate body.
Accept this spring of tears,
You who empty the seawater from the clouds.
Bend to the pain in my heart, You
who make the sky bend to your secret incarnation,
which emptied the heavens.
I will wash your feet with kisses
dry them with my hair, those feet whose steps
Eve heard at dusk in Paradise then hid in fear.
You who are limitless mercy – who will trace the results
of a lifetime I've done wrong, evaluate my weakness? I ask,
remember me,
if nothing else,
as one who
lived.

Mary Magdalene has come down to us as the woman with bowed head, with tears flowing past the fall of her hair: the Gospels' great sinner. But it seems that church fathers and believers alike made one story of three different women.

Mark and Luke tell of a nameless "woman of the city," a "sinner," who intruded on a meal Jesus was sharing with a Pharisee. The woman had brought an alabaster box of ointment, and she stood behind Jesus weeping as he sat at the table. She knelt, washed Jesus' feet, dried them with her long hair and kissed them, then spread the ointment on his feet. The Pharisee was disgusted that Jesus should let such a woman touch him, but Jesus rebuked his host. He had offered none of the signs of esteem that the woman had offered. Wordlessly, she had loved much, and she would be forgiven much. "Thy faith has saved thee," he told the woman. "Go in peace."

Mary of Bethany also anointed Jesus, but he knew her name well. She and her sister Martha and her brother Lazarus were dear friends of Jesus who invited him to their house. Mary sat at Jesus's feet, still and listening, while the resentful Martha cooked and served. "Make her help me," Martha complained, but Jesus praised Mary's spirit, which took the words from His mouth like food.

Later their brother fell ill; the sisters sent for Jesus, but Lazarus died. When Jesus arrived, he saw Mary bent with grief, and he wept and called her brother from the grave. Those who witnessed the miracle were astounded, and some spoke against him, so that the high priest declared Jesus would be arrested at Passover, if any knew where he was.

Six days before the Passover, even as Judas Iscariot plotted betrayal, Jesus and his disciples returned to Bethany. Martha served them, and Lazarus sat at table with the company. Their sister entered, carrying with her a precious spikenard ointment. This Mary knelt and with her long hair, she spread the oil on Jesus' feet until the house filled with its fragrance. Iscariot protested such extravagance, but Jesus silenced him. "Mary," he said, "has anointed me against the day of my burying."

Mary was a common name for women of this time. As for Mary of Magdala, called by name The Magdalene, the Gospels speak specifically of her in only two places. Jesus drove "seven devils" and "infirmities" out of her—and she stood by his mother's side during the dark vigil of the crucifixion. Mary Magdalene came to his tomb at dawn with spices for Jesus' torn body. Disturbed to see the stone rolled away from his sepulcher, she hurried to the disciples Peter and John. They followed her, but finding only the burial linens within an empty tomb, they left.

Mary Magdalene lingered, weeping. As she stooped down to look again into the tomb, two angels within asked her why she was crying. "Because they've taken him and I do not know where," she said and went back into the garden. There, meeting a man she believed to be the gardener, she begged, "Sir, tell me where you have laid him, and I will gladly take his body away."

The man called her name, *Mary*. Knowing Jesus' voice, she turned to him answering, *Master*, and looked into his living face.

"Touch me not," Jesus said to her, "for I am not yet ascended to my Father: but go to my brethren and say unto them, I ascend unto my Father and your Father; and to my God and your God." Mary Magdalene came and told the disciples that she had seen the Lord, and that he had spoken these things unto her.

Pope Gregory the Great cemented the blended image in 591, preaching, "She whom Luke calls the sinful woman, whom John calls Mary (of Bethany), we believe to be the Mary from whom seven devils were ejected according to Mark. And what did these seven devils signify if not all the vices. … It is clear, brothers, that the woman previously used the unguent to perfume her flesh in forbidden acts."

Forbidden acts. Thus the nameless sinner, contemplative Mary of Bethany, and Jesus' follower, Mary of Magdala, were painted as a single harlot by the highest authority. The Magdalene became a perfumed, forlorn figure any churchgoer could despise or pity, the suffering soul whose repentance and love redeemed her.

But in 1945, in upper Egypt near Nag Hammadi, two men unearthed a large jar that had been buried for fifteen hundred years. They found inside it thirteen leather-bound papyrus manuscripts. The owners of these early writings had hidden them well, perhaps from the burgeoning male hierarchy of the Church, certainly because they were valued. From several of these books, including The Gospel of Mary, another portrait of Mary Magdalene emerged, unseen for centuries. She was powerful among those closest to Jesus, a disciple, a questioner, and a teacher. "I want to understand all things," she said, "just as they are."

"There were three who always walked with the Lord," tells The Gospel of Philip: "Mary his mother and her sister and Magdalene, the one who was called his companion." Her prominence stirred jealousy among the disciples.

Peter in particular challenged her presence, demanding, "Did [Jesus] really speak to a woman without our knowledge [and] not openly? Are we to turn about and listen to her? Did he prefer her to us?"

Levi protested, "Peter, you have always been hot-tempered. Now I see you contending against the woman like the adversaries. But if the Savior made her worthy, who are you indeed to reject her? Surely the Savior knows her very well. That is why he loved her more than us."

"Why do you love her more than all of us?" they asked.

The Gospel of Philip records the savior's answer: "Why do I not love you like her? When a blind man and one who sees are both together in darkness, they are no different than one another. When the light comes, then he who sees will see the light, and he who is blind will remain in darkness." Mary Magdalene was the disciple able to see. She was, according to "The Dialogue of the Savior," "a woman who had understood completely."

In another ancient Gnostic text, the *Pistis Sophia*, Mary Magdalene sat with the disciples asking questions and offering interpretations. Here she was again opposed: "Peter leapt forward and said to Jesus: 'My Lord, we are not able to suffer this woman who takes the opportunity from us, and does not allow anyone of us to speak, but she speaks many times.'"

"Speak openly," Jesus said to her. "Thou art she whose heart is more directed to the Kingdom of Heaven than all thy brothers."

Because Jesus spoke first to her by the tomb, and it was she who told the disciples, the Eastern Orthodox Church has long named Mary Magdalene "The Apostle to the Apostles." During Holy Week, they sing the ninth-century female poet Kassia's hymn to her.

> Alas, what a desperate night I've traveled through.
>> Extravagant the desire, dark, and moonless
>> the needs of a passionate body.
> Accept this spring of tears,
>> You who empty the seawater from the clouds.
> Bend to the pain in my heart,
>> You who make the sky bend.

Kassia wrote her chant in the anguished voice of a "woman who fell into many sins." Now we know of the adept who "walked with the Lord," the full if embattled disciple, the lover of truth who wanted "to understand all things just as they are." Perhaps closer to the truth of Mary Magdalene is a line found in Proverbs: "She opens her mouth with wisdom and the teaching of kindness is on her tongue." And it is fair to plead, as Proverbs does:

> Give her a share in what her hands have made
>> Let her works tell her praises.

Anne

(1ˢᵗ century)
July 26

Mothers, Women in labor, Childless women, Miners, Cabinetmakers

"**A**nne" comes from the Hebrew "Hannah," meaning "favor" or "grace." Anne is not mentioned in the Bible, but in apocryphal Christian texts and in Islamic tradition, where she is named as the mother of Mary and thus, the grandmother of Jesus. The Protoevangelium, or Pre-gospel of James, thought to date from the second century, tells this story:

A holy day was approaching, and men brought offerings to the temple. Joachim, a wealthy man, brought twice as much as the others, but while their offerings were accepted, his were refused because he had fathered no children. Humiliated, he searched the registers of the twelve tribes to discover if he alone were the only childless man, and while searching, it came to him that God had given a son to Abraham in his old age. Joachim went out into the desert, fixed his tent and resolved to pray to the Lord for many days and nights until his prayer for a child was heard.

His wife Anne, after much waiting, believed herself a widow. She cried for Joachim and for having no child to lessen her gnawing loss. Her servant reproached her for mourning on a holy day. She offered Anne an ornate headband but Anne rejected it, saying she felt too low, and perhaps the person who had made it was wicked, and the ornament was cursed.

"Why should I curse you," murmured the servant, "when your womb is already cursed?"

At these words, Anne felt emptiness all through herself and around her on every side. Because it was the holy day, though, she changed her widow's dress for her wedding clothes, washed her face, brushed her hair, and went away from the servant into her garden.

There she sank down under a laurel tree. Catching sight of a sparrow's nest in the laurel, Anne cried, "What am I? I am not like the birds of the earth because I have no child. I am not like the beasts because I have no child. I am not like the waters or the earth itself, for everything flowers and multiplies but I have not." Then she too remembered Abraham and his wife Sarah and the gift of their son, Isaac, in their old age, and she prayed the same prayer as her husband in the desert.

An angel stood beside her, saying, "Anne, Anne, the Lord has heard your prayer, and you shall conceive, and shall bring forth: and your seed shall be spoken of in all the world." Anne vowed that any child she might have, male or female, would all its life serve the Lord. "Go now to meet your husband at the gate," the angel said, "for he is coming with his flocks."

Out in the desert, an angel stood beside Joachim and told him his wife would conceive. Joachim hurried to find his shepherds, telling them to pick ten perfect lambs, twelve calves, and a hundred goats for the people, and he drove the animals in front of him. His wife was waiting at the gate. Anne flung her arms around her husband, and they went home together.

Later Joachim made his offerings for a second time, watching the priest

61

anxiously. This time the priest accepted what he had given, and Joachim was strengthened and felt himself a man of his tribe. Some months later, Anne gave birth to the baby the angel promised. She asked, "What is my child?"

"A girl," said the midwife.

Anne's soul sang within her, and she called her daughter Mary.

Pascual Baylon

(1540-1592)
May 17

Cooks, Kitchens, Kitchen workers, Finding lost domestic animals, Cheeriness

SAN PASQUAL
PATRON OF COOKS AND KITCHENS

Pascual's parents, Martin Baylon and Elizabeth Jubera, were Spanish peasants who sent their son to the fields as a shepherd. Only seven, the boy carried a book along with him so that he could persuade anyone who passed by to teach him to read it. Once he had learned, he immersed himself in religious books and in prayer while his parents' sheep wandered farther and farther away.

Pascual was born in Aragon during the Pentecost or "The Pasch of the Holy Ghost" and named for that holy day. Saying, "I was born poor and am resolved to die in poverty and penance," he chose a simple, meditative life. The Franciscan order accepted him as a lay brother in 1564.

Pascual was a cheerful man whose counsel was sought by people of every station, and he was particularly tender to the sick and the poor. He was devoted to the Sacrament and often knelt before the monstrance for long hours in the night. A story tells that on one of these nights his Franciscan brothers came upon him flushed and dancing at the altar, an ecstasy of light radiating from his body.

But legend puts him in the monastery's kitchen, for Pascual is known as the patron of cooks. Zabaione, a dish of egg yolks whipped with sugar and wine, was said to be an invention of his. The recipe for this fluffy pudding was easily remembered as 1+2+2+1: Pascual the cook mixed one egg yolk with two spoonfuls of sugar, two eggshells of wine, and, ever mindful of the poor who could not afford so much wine, one eggshell of water.

As was his custom, he prayed as he worked. Thus angels hovered nearby to save Pascual's sweet custard from burning.

Martha

(1st century)
July 29

Servers, Cooks, Housewives, Housekeepers, Hotel keepers, Laundry workers

Martha of Bethany is the Bible's famous housekeeper, sister to Mary and Lazarus. The Gospel of Luke tells that when Jesus visited their house, Martha bustled about preparing a meal while her sister Mary sat still at Jesus' feet and fed her spirit on his words.

Martha raised her voice, saying, "Lord, do you not care that my sister has left all the serving to me? Tell her to help me."

"Martha, Martha," Jesus answered, "you are troubled about many things—but one thing is necessary. Mary has chosen the good part, and that shall not be taken away from her."

The Gospel of John tells that Martha and Mary sent for Jesus, saying, "Our brother, whom you love, is sick." Hearing this, Jesus said to his disciples that his friend Lazarus' sickness was an occasion to reveal the glory of God, to make unbelievers believe. He set out for Bethany two days later, but by the time he drew near, Lazarus had already lain four days in the grave.

Martha hurried out to meet Jesus. "Lord," she said, "if you had been here my brother would not have died. But I know that even now, whatever you ask of God, God will give to you."

Jesus said, "Martha, your brother will live again."

"I know that he will rise again on the resurrection in the last day."

"I am the resurrection and the life," Jesus said. "He that believes in me, even though he is dead, will live. And whoever lives and believes in me shall never die. Do you believe this?"

"Yes, Lord, I believe that you are the Son of God who came into the world."

She went back to her house. Perhaps, after the first visit, the industrious Martha had interrupted her tasks so that her sister could repeat all that Jesus had said, for she at once told Mary that he had arrived and was calling for her.

Mary ran to him in the road and threw herself down. "Lord, if you had been here, my brother would not have died."

Her tears hurt Jesus deep in his spirit, for he loved these three. "Where have you laid him?"

When they came to the tomb, a cave shut with a stone, Jesus wept for Lazarus. Some onlookers remarked how dearly Jesus cared for Lazarus; others wondered, if he can heal the blind, why did he not save his friend?

"Take away the stone," Jesus said.

Practical Martha protested that the body would smell, for her brother had been dead four days.

"Did not I tell you that if you believed you would see God's power?"

The stone was rolled away. Jesus lifted his eyes, and so that the people gathered there would believe that God sent him, that God worked through him, he thanked his Father aloud for hearing him. But he knew his Father heard him always.

He cried out, "Lazarus, come forth!"

Wound in his grave clothes, Lazarus walked living out of the tomb.

The Gospel of John tells one last story in which Martha appears. Six days before Passover Jesus returned to Bethany for a supper. Lazarus sat at table with the company. Mary carried in a pound of precious spikenard oil and knelt as before at Jesus' feet. She rubbed on the amber oil then wiped his feet with her hair; all the while, the house grew fragrant with earthy perfume.

As for Mary's sister, John records, "Martha served."

The Golden Legend names Martha the hostess and Jesus the Guest. The tales in this medieval compilation give Martha a royal background and, after the Crucifixion, send her and her sister and brother to France on a raft without a sail.

There Martha preached, converting the people all around. She even battled a dragon, "half-animal and half-fish, larger than an ox, longer than a horse, with teeth as sharp as horns," that was eating a man until she subdued it with a cross and holy water.

When Martha's death approached, she asked those close to her to light lamps and keep vigil with her. But they fell asleep, and wind blew out the lamps. Martha's sister Mary, who had already passed, came to her with a torch and lit all the lamps and many candles, and the two sisters spoke each other's names.

Jesus came then, saying, "Come, beloved hostess, where I am, there will you be with me." The hostess had welcomed the Guest into her house. Now, amidst the burning lamps and candle-flames, the Guest welcomed the hostess into his heaven.

Luke

(1st century)
October 18

Artists, Doctors, Surgeons, Sculptors, Brewers, Glassworkers, Goldsmiths

Luke, who accompanied the apostle Paul in his ministry, was a doctor, possibly an artist, from the city of Antioch. Many scholars believe he wrote The Acts of the Apostles as well as the Gospel named for him. Both books start with a salutation to Theophilus, perhaps a friend, or simply a fellow Christian, for the name means "lover of God." Luke himself was not a disciple; he took his account from those who "from the beginning were eyewitnesses."

Luke's narrative holds songs and, in greater number than any other Gospel, stories of the women important to Jesus. First it tells of the barren Elisabeth, cousin to Mary and wife to elderly temple priest Zacharias. Archangel Gabriel announces to Zacharias that the priest will soon be father of a son named John. When Zacharias dares to question whether his old wife can conceive, the archangel renders him mute.

Before Elisabeth's child is born, Gabriel appears also to her young cousin. Mary's question—how will she conceive when she has not known a man—Gabriel does not refuse to answer: "the Highest shall overshadow thee … and the child shall be the Son of God." Mary pays a visit to Elisabeth, and the child who will become John the Baptist leaps in Elisabeth's womb, in greeting of the child Jesus that Mary carries. The inspired, older woman pronounces Mary and the fruit of her womb blessed, and Mary sings her agreement in a canticle of praise, only in The Gospel of Luke. Once Elisabeth is delivered, and her husband has confirmed their child's name, John, on a tablet, his voice is restored. Zacharias, full of a father's hope, sings a hymn to a son who will "give light to them that sit in darkness … and guide our feet into the way of peace."

"Peace and good will toward men," the angels sing to the shepherds on the night Jesus is born. These men search out the child and Joseph and Mary in a manger and afterward spread the joyful tidings across the countryside. Luke's Gospel turns from the noisy celebration to note that the new mother "kept all these things and pondered them in her heart." Twelve years later, Mary encounters the strange profundity of her son as well as a hint of his death when Jesus is discovered in the temple teaching the teachers, and again she tucks away "all these sayings in her heart."

The Gospel of Matthew counts Jesus' heritage back to the Jewish patriarch Abraham, but Luke's Gospel lengthens it, naming back to the universal father Adam, suggesting that his writings are open to all who will accept them.

The two Gospels differ further. Matthew's sets down the journey of the regal Easterners who brought the child Jesus frankincense and gold; Luke's offers the humble shepherds in the fields. It relates the favorite parables of the Prodigal Son and of the Good Samaritan, who saves a "half dead" stranger lying in the road while other people hustle past. As Jesus confronts his own death in the garden of Gethsemane, he is "sorrowful and very heavy" according to Matthew. Luke's image prefigures Jesus' agony: "his sweat was as … great drops of blood falling down to the ground."

In The Acts, the apostles preach Jesus' life and creed, work miracles in his name, and, for his sake, suffer persecution. Judges, perceiving an angel in Stephen's face, still order him stoned; this first Christian martyr dies shouting for Jesus to receive his spirit. James the Greater is put to death by the sword on Herod's command. Peter heals a lame man huddled at a gate called "Beautiful," he brings the seamstress Tabitha back from the dead, and he is beaten and imprisoned, again and again. The disciples' bitterest enemy is Saul. He threatens to destroy them and the words of Christ—until Jesus' voice waylays him on the road to Damascus, throws Saul down in a blinding light, and changes him heart and spine. The new man standing up from that road takes the name Paul and becomes the greatest of Jesus' apostles.

The audience for Christianity widens in The Acts. Here Paul preaches that God "hath made of one blood all nations of men for to dwell on the face of the earth." Jesus has chosen Paul to carry his "name before the Gentiles, and kings, and children of Israel." Indeed, King Herod Agrippa decides, "I should like to hear the man myself." After Paul unfolds the story of his dramatic conversion, Agrippa says, "Almost thou persuadest me to be a Christian."

Paul closed one of his letters with "Luke, the beloved physician, and Demas, greet you," for Luke was often by his side. Luke recorded Paul's arrests and trials, the miracles and the calamitous voyages. Shore after shore, the names rolled from his pen: Troas, Chios, Samos, Ephesus, Rhodes, Cypress, Syria, Tyre, finally Rome.

Paul wrote his last letter, to Timothy, from a Roman prison: "The time of my departure is at hand. I have fought the good fight, I have finished the race, I have kept the faith. Do your best to come to me soon. For Demas, in love with this present world, has forsaken me, and gone to Thessalonica, Crescens has gone to Galatia, Titus to Dalmatia. Only Luke is with me."

Matthew

(1ˢᵗ century)
September 21

Accountants, Bankers, Bookkeepers, Stockbrokers, Tax collectors, Money managers,
Security guards, Customs officials

St. Matthew

The Gospel of Matthew traces Jesus' lineage back forty-two generations, from Joseph through Solomon and David to the patriarch Abraham. It recounts his birth, how his stepfather Joseph guarded him from bloody King Herod, his baptism, and how he fasted alone in the wilderness. There he encountered the blandishments of Satan, but flung him back.

By the Sea of Galilee, Jesus called as disciples the fishermen Peter, Andrew, James the Greater, and John, who set down their nets and went with him. He preached the mighty Sermon on the Mount to crowds and passed among them healing. Then, across the water, he walked into Capernaum and saw a tax collector, one of a shunned class of people, sitting at his table in the customhouse. "Follow me," Jesus said. Matthew got up at once, leaving on the table his accounts and stacks of coins, and followed him.

The tax collector laid a feast at his house, and others of his profession, scorned as agents of imperial Rome, sat at table with Jesus. Someone implored the disciples, "Why does your Master eat with tax collectors and sinners?" Jesus heard and answered, "I am not come to call the righteous but sinners."

Matthew, also named Levi, accompanied Jesus as one of his disciples. To these twelve Jesus spoke at length so that they would understand the formidable nature of their choice.

They would have the power to heal and to drive out evil. They would travel empty-handed, trusting to find food and shelter on the road; they would bring peace to the houses that welcomed them and as for those that did not, they were to leave those houses, shaking the dust off their feet, and find others. They would be like sheep in a land of wolves; they would be hated and persecuted. What he told them among their own circle, they would preach upon housetops.

Jesus warned the disciples that their devotion to him tolerated no provisions. His revolutionary message would divide houses: set son against father or daughter-in-law against mother-in-law; if they could not love him more than their own family, they were not worthy to be his disciples. But whoever accepted them also accepted Jesus; whoever, for the sake of a disciple, gave even a cup of cold water to a child would be rewarded by Jesus himself.

Matthew and the others shared the years of Jesus' traveling and preaching. The disciples gave out the endless loaves and fishes, witnessed his miracles and heard him praised and reviled. They wondered, they questioned, they failed in understanding. They mulled over the metaphors of his parables, and they sealed his words into their hearts; they stayed near him until the night one of their own, Judas Iscariot, sold Jesus into the hands of the Romans.

Eleven disciples lingered as their teacher was delivered to Pontius Pilate and then to the cross. On Golgotha that long day the disciples watched, and they listened as he cried out to his Father and died.

The Gospel of Matthew tells that Mary Magdalene and another Mary, coming to take his broken body, found the tomb empty except for an angel, who bade them to go to the disciples and say that Jesus had risen from death, and that they would see him in Galilee. There, on a mountain, Jesus commissioned them as his apostles: they should go out and teach the nations what they had learned from him.

Surely his last promise, as Matthew recorded it, sustained these people who faced such a fraught task, such an uncharted road ahead of them. "I am with you always," Jesus said, "even unto the end of the world."

Matthew preached in Judea and possibly in Ethiopia, Persia, and the kingdom of the Parthians. Some ancient historians contended that he was killed for his faith. Others found little evidence to add "martyr" to the list of what Matthew was: despised tax collector, chosen disciple, apostle, and evangelist, writer of the Gospel that opens the New Testament.

Archangel Gabriel

September 29

Media, Communications workers, Postal workers

Gabriel

One of the dreamers of the Old Testament, Daniel, looked up and saw a man "clothed in linen, whose loins were girded with fine gold of Uphaz. His body also was like the beryl, and his face as the appearance of lightning, and his eyes as lamps of fire, and his arms and his feet like in color to polished brass and the voice of his words like the voice of a multitude."

Daniel fell down, afraid. But this being of lightning and fire said to him, "Fear not, Daniel, for from the first day that thou didst set thine heart to understand and to chasten thyself before thy God, thy words were heard, and I am come for thy words." Daniel recounted his strange visions, and Gabriel, God's messenger, revealed their meaning.

In The Gospel of Luke, an angel brought news of two births. First, he came to the priest Zacharias to tell him his barren wife Elisabeth would at last conceive a son. The child should be called John, and he would be "great in the sight of the Lord."

"How can I know such a thing?" asked Zacharias. "I am an old man, and my wife is old, past her childbearing years."

"I am Gabriel that stands in the presence of God," said the angel, "sent to give you this good news. Since you did not believe me, you shall be not able to speak until the day these things come to be."

Zacharias found that his throat was locked, and when he went into the street he could not answer those who greeted him.

Then Gabriel, beryl and gold, was sent to Mary, the betrothed of the Nazarene carpenter, Joseph. He delivered this message, "Blessed art thou among women. You have found favor with God, and you will bear His son. The child's name shall be Jesus, and of his kingdom there shall be no end."

It happened as the angel said. Elisabeth's son was born, and the neighbors would have called the son after his father. But mute Zacharias scratched the boy's name, John, on a tablet, and afterward his voice returned to him.

Mary's child, Jesus, was born in Bethlehem, the city of David, where she and her husband Joseph had traveled to be counted. In the fields nearby lay shepherds who cried out when an angel spoke to them from a column of light.

Again, the angel told them not to fear. "I bring you good tidings of great joy which shall be to all people. For unto you is born this day in the city of David a Saviour which is Christ the Lord." Many more angels joined this one, and they sang peace and good will down on the earth, the chorus of their voices as joyous as a father's who has seen his child for the first time.

And Gabriel the messenger climbed back through the night sky, going home.

Archangel Michael

September 29

Warriors, Police officers, EMTs, Paratroopers, Fighter pilots, Grocers, Radiologists, Cancer

Commander of the armies of God, protector of the children of Israel, leader of souls to judgment and reward, healer: the archangel Michael can be found in the texts and traditions of many cultures.

In the Hebrew Book of Enoch, Michael was set over the worthiest of mankind; "patient and merciful," his was the "first voice" that "blesses the Lord of Spirits forever and ever." He instructed Enoch that those who loved God would be glad.

> And into the holy place shall they enter;
> And its fragrance shall be in their bones,
> And they shall live a long life on earth,
> Such as thy fathers lived:
> And in their days shall no sorrow or plague
> Or torment or calamity touch them.

Jewish lore made Michael the angel who spoke to Moses from the burning bush and delivered to the patriarch the tablets on Mount Sinai, and the angel who visited Moses' general, Joshua, as he prepared to fight for Jericho and the promised lands. Joshua looked up to see a man "with his sword drawn in his hand" and asked him, "Are you with us or with our enemies?" The armed man answered, "Nay, as captain of the host of the Lord am I now come."

Fathers of the Christian church claimed Michael as the angel who guided the Israelites out of Egypt, appearing by day as a pillar of cloud and by night as a pillar of fire; the angel who walked with Shadrach, Meshach, and Abednego through the fiery furnace, so that they had "no hurt"; the angel who brought food to Daniel when he was shut fast into the lions' den.

Michael's name is first written in the Bible in the Book of Daniel. The archangel Gabriel told Daniel that he had been engaged in battle for one hundred and twenty days and "there is none that holdeth with me in these things but Michael, your prince." Further, the angel prophesied about the end of days when Michael would "stand up, the great prince which standeth for the children of thy people and … thy people shall be delivered, every one that shall be found written in the book."

In the Book of Jude, Michael disputed with the devil over the body of Moses, which he hid, for Satan would have delighted in tempting men and women to worship it as an idol.

In the vision of Revelation, St. John the Divine saw Michael lead the sons of light against the sons of darkness and their chief, Satan, who assumed the form of a seven-headed dragon.

> There was war in heaven: Michael and his angels fought
> against the dragon; and the dragon fought and his angels,
> And prevailed not; neither was their place found anymore in

heaven. And the great dragon was cast out, that old serpent called the Devil, and Satan, which deceiveth the whole world: he was cast out into the earth and his angels were cast out with him.

"Mich-a-el" is translated in the Talmudic tradition as "Who is like God?" The name is not a question meant to be answered, but a battle cry. The angels taunted Satan, "Michael! Michael! Who is like God!" as they struck down his forces. They rebuked the devil for his presumption until he had tumbled from the light into the darker air.

The invocation of Michael as healing spirit may have begun at Colossae, where he was said to have thwarted pagans who directed a stream against his chapel. The archangel sent lightning to split a boulder, clearing a new bed for the stream, and he sanctified its waters so that the sick who bathed there were cured. At Constantinople, the ill and the lame passed nights in his sanctuary, praying and waiting for the angel to appear.

Egyptian Christians made Michael the patron of the Nile and dedicated a feast to him at the season the great river began to rise. To the Greeks, he was the guide of souls to the afterlife, and only the dead and those near death could see his face.

Islamic lore has it that Michael's wings are "the color of green emerald ... covered with saffron hairs, each of them containing a million faces and mouths and as many tongues which, in a million dialects, implore the pardon of Allah."

Knights of medieval times chose this archangel as their guiding figure, and in 1511, King James IV of the Scots launched the largest ship on the ocean, a four-masted, thousand-ton carrack called *Great Michael*.

Many people today call on St. Michael to aid them in their battle against cancer. He is known as the protector of the sick, of grocers, seafarers, police officers, EMTs, and paratroopers. *"Oración a San Miguel Arcangel,"* the prayer of the 42nd Infantry Brigade, Paratroopers of Venezuela, asks St. Michael, *"cuídame de los enemigos silenciosos y ayúdame a ser justo para que ... a nadie ofenda, ni resienta, y por contrario, viva en paz con los hombres, para llegar dignamente a Dios."*

> Saint Michael, protect me against silent enemies
> and help me to be just
> so that I may neither offend nor resent anyone
> so that I may live in peace
> so that I may arrive worthy before God
> Amen.

Catherine of Alexandria

(early 4th century)
November 25

Young women, Students, Spinners, Wheelwrights, Millers, Philosophers,
Preachers, Teachers

Sor Juana de la Cruz, seventeenth-century nun, writer, and an intellectual embattled with the male religious authorities of her time, cherished the third century's Catherine of Alexandria. The refrain of one of Sor Juana's villancicos, or Spanish carols, praised Catherine: "Yes, this is what it means to shine!" In another, she sang knowingly:

> Because if there's one thing
> That drives the devil up a tree
> it's hearing of a woman
> who is smarter than he.

Eighteen-year-old Catherine heard that the emperor Maxentius had ordered the Christians to sacrifice to idols. Fearing their deaths, the Christians were about to obey when Catherine entered the pagan temple. *The Golden Legend* of Jacobus de Voragine tells that the young girl argued with Maxentius by means of syllogism, allegory, metaphor, and logic. Then she simply asked him why he commanded the people to worship stupid idols.

Why worship artisans' gems and ornaments that in time will crumble to sand and drift away? He should instead be awed by land and rolling seas, by *their* ornaments—sun, moon, and stars and their eternal routes across the sky—and he should ask himself who is more powerful than these. Then he would know God and adore Him.

Discomposed by this bold girl, Maxentius sent her to his palace. He soon followed and after tendering his admiration for her knowledge, demanded to know of her parents.

Catherine told him that one should neither speak grandly nor disparage oneself, for both those impulses spring from a desire for that thin cape, glory. She was the daughter of King Costus, "born to the purple," well educated, but she had turned away to find a truer shelter in Lord Jesus Christ.

"Your carved idols, Maxentius—call their names when you are in need or in danger. They cannot help you, for they are hollow."

"So you say that everyone in the world is wrong," the emperor bellowed, "and you alone know the truth?"

"Watch lest anger overwhelm wisdom," said Catherine. "For the poet has written, 'If you are ruled by the mind, you are a king, if by the body, you are a slave.'"

The emperor summoned to the court fifty master philosophers and promised them riches if they could talk the girl silent. "Why, even our apprentices could refute a woman," they scoffed. The emperor brought Catherine into their presence, and with an angel at her back, she came to debate them.

"A god cannot become a man. A god cannot suffer," said the philosophers.

"But Plato wrote of a god mutilated," Catherine reminded them, and she quoted the sybil who spoke this oracle, "'Happy that God who hangs from a high tree!'"

The master philosophers tried another tact, but the girl answered them. The debate ranged on, but they could not confound her in learning or in conviction, and one by one each became afraid to speak. Finally, they affirmed to Maxentius that they themselves would desert idols and follow the God this girl championed. Enraged, the emperor had a fire heaped up in the middle of Alexandria and the fifty philosophers thrown into it.

Next he tried a lure: Catherine should join him in his palace, ranking only below his wife the queen.

Catherine responded at once. The emperor should not speak this way, for she had given herself to her lover and sweet bridegroom, Christ.

Maxentius had her shut away and starved. But the queen and the captain of the emperor's guard, Porphyrius, visited her. In her cell washed by light, Catherine converted these two, and, crowded outside her door, the soldiers of the emperor's guard bent their knees.

Maxentius ordered his carpenters to build a terrible instrument, four wheels fit with iron saws and spikes, two turning right, two turning left, meant to tear apart Catherine and to terrify Christians. But when Catherine's hand touched the wheel, spikes and saws flew off, and the machine itself splintered into bits of wood and iron.

At this, the queen pleaded for the girl and was carried outside the city and put to death. Porphyrius of the guard found the queen's body and buried her. He strode before the emperor, reported that he had buried the queen, then that he himself had become Christian.

"Even you," said Maxentius, who then appealed to the soldiers of the guard.

The men answered him that they too were Christians and prepared to die.

The desperate emperor held out his last bribe to Catherine: if she would come to her senses, she should rule as queen in his palace.

She refused. "Do anything you can think of," the girl told him. "I can bear whatever it is."

Just before Catherine was beheaded, a voice was heard calling her to the Beloved she prayed to and had wisely spoken for. Legend has it that milk rather than blood spilled from her neck.

Sor Juana de la Cruz asserted that "Even God in the world finds no loves without danger." She wrote of her sister Catherine of Alexandria:

> She studies, she argues and teaches
> all in the service of the church
> since the one who gave her the gift of reason
> did not mean for her to be ignorant.

John of the Cross

(1542-1591)
December 14

Contemplative life, Mystics, Spanish poets

SAN JUAN de la CRUZ

"Where there is no love, put love," said John of the Cross, "and you will find love."

Juan de Yepes y Alvarez was born in Fontiveros, Spain, to a father who had been disinherited when he married for love a silk weaver's daughter. After his father died, the family knew desperate poverty. John joined the order of the Carmelites in 1563, though he doubted his strength for the priesthood. Then he met Teresa de Ávila, the powerful reformer who was spreading the ways of the Discalced Carmelites throughout Spain.

Tireless, charismatic, a mystic, she recognized the same light in the young priest who named himself John of the Cross. She persuaded him to remain and support her work; in time she made him confessor and director of the Convent of the Incarnation. It was some of the many opponents to her reform that kidnapped John of the Cross in December of 1577 and locked him in a Toledo prison room.

His cell measured six feet by ten. One small, high window admitted feeble light. The monks jailed and starved him in numbing cold followed by summer's smothering heat. Weekly his captors took him down to their refectory where they whipped him during their dinner hour. When he did not cry out, they accused him further. Friendless, spoken against, bloody and scarred and tempted to give in, John of the Cross went down into a dark night.

This long dark night wore away reason, will, and senses. Memory and imagination failed to comfort; it seemed that even prayers could not pass the thick stone walls. His soul emptied: it knew nothing, it was nothing. "I went out of myself," he wrote.

John of the Cross told his soul's story in verses he kept by memory. Not until a guard softened by the prisoner's patient nature slipped him ink, quill, and scroll could he write out his verses in the shadow of his cell. He stuffed these into pockets when, after nine months, he found a chance to escape. He lowered himself by a rope made of twisted cloth onto the ground outside the monastery and made his way to a convent of Teresa's nuns. The sisters were singing the Angelus; their voices floated outside to John of the Cross as he wept against the wall of their chapel.

Out of that captivity and an ecstatic state afterward sprang his enduring poems and commentaries defining the soul's dangerous journey. In "*En un Noche Oscura*," he told how, guided only by a lover's burning longing for God, he made his way from a quietened house alone. He blessed the dark, secret night he walked through, surer than the light of noon, lovelier than dawn, for within its emptiness he met his Beloved. He laid his face against Him, and all ceased then—world, senses, self. "My cares," he wrote, "I left among the lilies, forgotten."

"Do not be surprised if I show a great love of suffering," John of the Cross said. "God gave me a high idea of its value when I was in prison in Toledo."

That place was not his last prison. He spent the months before his death mistreated by the harsh, jealous Prior of Ubeda. John's humility eventually caused his foul keeper to be stricken with remorse. Thus his friends were joined around him the night that John of the Cross murmured, "Into your hands, Beloved, I commend my spirit" and went free into the dark and the stillness.

The Virgin of Guadalupe

December 12

Mexico, The Americas, Bread-making, The afflicted, Remedy for all ills

In 1531 in Mexico, an Indian peasant walked out before dawn, wrapped in a coarse maguey cloak, or tilma, for warmth. His native name was *Cuauhtlatoatzin*, Eagle who Talks; his Christian name was Juan Diego. It was a Saturday in December, the time of frost.

The sun began to rise as he came to the hill of Tepeyac, where he heard throngs of birds singing. Their singing left off, and the hill itself seemed to offer a song in return, calmer and softer than the choir of the birds. Transfixed, Juan Diego wondered why a humble soul like himself heard such sounds. Maybe he was dreaming? Maybe without knowing he had passed into the land of flowers and maize, the land of his grandfathers?

The hill's song finished, and someone called to him, "Juanito, Juan Dieguito." Filled with peace, he walked toward the voice, and saw a woman who asked him to come closer. The rising sun shimmered her in rays of light. The mesquite and prickly pears that grew all around her gleamed emerald and turquoise, and their thorns were gold. He fell down before her and she spoke to him.

"Listen, my son, the youngest, Juanito, where are you headed?"

Juan Diego answered, "My lady, my queen, my little girl, I am going to your home in Mexico-Tlatelolco to follow the ways of God."

The woman told him she was the Virgin Holy Mary. "I am the compassionate mother, " she said, "yours and of all men who are united on this land. And of all the other different races of men; those who love me, those who cry out for me, those who seek me, those who trust me, because I will listen to their weeping." She wished him to go to the Bishop of Mexico and tell him to build her a house on this hill.

Juan Diego replied that he, a poor Indian, would hurry to carry out what she had asked him to do. He went straight to Mexico, and in that city found the palace of the Bishop, a Franciscan named Juan de Zumárraga. He waited there for a long time before being brought to the bishop, and then he told the Franciscan father all that he had seen on the hill of Tepeyac. The bishop heard him out, then said that Juan Diego should come again.

Disappointed that he had not been able to carry out the Virgin's commission straightaway, Juan Diego returned to Tepeyac, where he found the Queen of Heaven waiting. He bowed down. It seemed to him that the bishop doubted his message; Juan Diego asked her to send a more credible person to speak to the bishop, a noble, someone respected, "for I am only a man of the land; a handcart, a lowly man, a wing; I myself must be led, carried; the place where you send me is no place for me."

The Virgin assured him that she did not lack for servants to do her will, but she had chosen him, and she asked him to go again the next day to the bishop.

Juan Diego walked home to sleep, and on the next morning, a Sunday, he went to Tlatelolco to mass and afterward to the palace of the Bishop. He begged to see him, and he waited, and finally escorted to Bishop Zumárraga, he knelt at his feet. Juan Diego repeated the Virgin's, the Lady's, the Queen of Heaven's request, and he wept. The bishop questioned him but would not take his word, and asked him to bring a sign that what he had said was true.

Servants of the bishop followed Juan Diego on his way home, but they lost him near a wooden bridge by Tepeyac. They searched, and not finding him, returned to the bishop and condemned Juan Diego as a liar.

But Juan Diego was speaking once more with the Lady on the hill, telling her of the sign he was requested to bring. She promised him the sign on the next day.

On that day, a Monday, Juan Diego's uncle, Juan Bernardino, fell ill of the plague. The nephew brought a doctor who did what he could, but Juan Bernardino was past curing. Then the uncle asked his nephew for a priest, for he would not rise again in this world, and he wanted to give his confession.

In the early, dark hours of Tuesday, Juan Diego left his uncle's house to fetch a priest from Tlatelolco. So urgent was his uncle's plea that Juan Diego in his haste skirted the hill of Tepeyac. The Virgin saw, and she came down the hill to him.

Afraid, ashamed, Juan Diego knelt in her sunlight. He told her that he was hurrying to find a priest for his dying uncle, but as soon as this duty was done, he would rush back to her at Tepeyac.

The Virgin answered, "Listen, put this in your heart, my son, the youngest … am I, your mother, not here? Are you not under my shadow and my protection? Are you not in the hollow of my mantle, in the crossing of my arms? Do you need more?" She told him that his uncle was well now. As for the sign, Juan Diego should climb to the crest of the hill, where he had first seen her. There he should gather flowers and return to her.

This was not a hill on which flowers grew; it was the rocky home of mesquite, thistle, cactus, and thorn. But Juan Diego rose, and wrapping his tilma closer around him against the thin, winter-sharp air, with frost crackling underfoot and the ice of stars overhead, he climbed the hill.

On reaching the top, Juan Diego found a profusion of blooming flowers, their petals open and fragrant in the cold night. He cut many and carried them back down to the Lady, who placed them in his tilma with her own hands.

Juan Diego took the road, happy in his heart, believing now that he could carry out this divine request. He reached the palace before dawn and pleaded with the servants to call the bishop, but not a one of them budged. The servants mocked Juan Diego by acting as though they could not understand the words from his mouth.

They sidled near him, though, once the bundle concealed within his tilma had aroused their curiosity. The servants were agog at the sight of the unseasonal flowers, at their freshness and delicate scents—but when they tried to grasp them, they could no longer see them. The servants ran then and called the bishop. Hearing of the flowers, Bishop Zumárraga realized that this was the sign he had asked for.

He came down to meet Juan Diego, who unfolded his cloak, and as the flowers dropped to the floor, there appeared on the rough-fibered tilma the image of the Virgin who spoke to Juan Diego on the hill at Tepeyac, the woman with the circle of light behind her body and the radiance of the sun and the moon.

Bishop Zumárraga knelt and asked her pardon for not carrying out her will at once, and he placed the tilma with her image in his chapel. A day later a large party traveled to see the hill where the Queen of Heaven wished her shrine to stand, and then Juan Diego asked permission to return to his uncle.

The bishop and his party accompanied Juan Diego to his uncle's home. Juan Bernardino, well and strong now, bewildered to find such important people at his door, turned to his nephew, who related the story of the Virgin and her promise that the uncle was cured even as they spoke.

It is true, said Juan Bernardino, for as he trembled and struggled to breathe, the image of a radiant woman had appeared to him, and told him that his illness was gone; told him all that she had asked of his nephew, and her name, which was The Virgin Mary of Guadalupe.

Juan Diego's tilma was placed in the main church where the people of Mexico journeyed to see the vibrant image of Guadalupe, to offer to her their devotion and prayers, and to draw from her strength and love.

A Spanish account of these miraculous appearances in Mexico was published by the priest Miguel Sanchez in 1648. The retelling above, however, is taken from the *Nican Mopohua*, meaning "Thus, She speaks." This story passed from mouth to mouth until it was recorded, perhaps by Mexican-born scholar Antonio Valeriano, perhaps by sanctuary chaplain Luis Lasso de la Vega, who published it in a book in 1649.

The *Nican Mopohua* was written in Nahuatl, the language in which La Virgin María de Guadalupe spoke to Juan Diego for he, *Cuauhtlatoatzin*, Eagle Who Talks, was Indian, and that was his language.

Librada

(3ʳᵈ century)
July 30

Women wishing to be free of bad husbands and boyfriends, Women in labor, Strong women, Prostitutes, Criminals, Helpers at time of death, Bearded women

Librada, the female counterpart of the crucified Christ, is a mythical saint who became a martyr by defying her father's wishes. Legend places her in the third century, one of seven or nine daughters born of a single birth to a Portuguese queen. Young Librada, desiring for herself a life of prayer and contemplation, accordingly vowed to remain a virgin.

However, she was a striking girl, and her father ambitious. He ordered her married to the king of Sicily, a match that stood to bring him greater riches and power. Librada prayed to be saved from this union she did not want.

Her prayers were answered when a beard sprouted on her tender face, and the king of Sicily hastily withdrew his offer. Enraged at a daughter who would pursue her own will, her father the King of Portugal had Librada crucified.

It is believed that St. Librada was the result of confusion over popular prints of the cross of Lucca, well known to pilgrims of the twelfth century, which depicted Jesus in a flowing robe and royal crown. Mistaking the gowned figure for a woman, people began to call her the Vierge-Forte, or Strong Virgin.

The people of Holland called her "the one who takes away grief." She was named Uncumber in England, where women burdened with cumbersome husbands and lovers asked her help to be freed of them. Sir Thomas More, canonized himself four hundred years later, remarked that women of London were much seen in St. Paul's Cathedral, beseeching this image of the girl on the cross.

Thus people made of the saint what they needed of her, and Librada became the patron of women of strength and conviction.

Her name, so suggestive of liberation, has only extended her powers of protection. A hand-written note found at the *Santuario de Chimayó* in New Mexico instructs:

> Pray to Librada
> in times of trouble with the police and the courts
> She will help you if you believe
> Pray to Librada
> when your freedom is not visible.

Expeditus

(early 4th century)
April 19

Emergencies, Prompt solutions, Procrastination,
Computer programmers and hackers, E-commerce

SAN EXPEDITO

Roman emperor Diocletian set out in 303 to cleanse his empire of Christians in the usual bloody way: kill them. A list compiled on April 19 at the killing grounds of Melitene, now Malatya, Turkey, includes the name "Expeditus." No details of the man's life exist, only this note of his death. Perhaps this faceless soldier was of the class of fighter known as "expeditus," the ones who marched lightly armed, unburdened by a pack, for he is said to have been a Roman centurion who bowed his knee to Christ.

Legend tells that on the day of his conversion, the devil took the shape of a crow and cawed at him, "Wait until tomorrow to be Christian."

Expeditus ground the bird beneath his foot, saying, "I will be a Christian today!"

Though location varies—Paris, New Orleans, Reunion Island—the story behind the cult of Expeditus remains remarkably the same. A group of nuns received a box thought to contain relics of an unknown saint. The senders had marked it "Spedito" or "Expedit" so that the box would be quickly delivered. The nuns, however, took this marking for the name of the saint and petitioned him for some pressing favors. When these were swiftly granted, Saint Expeditus' reputation was launched.

It flourishes around the world, especially in New Orleans and in Brazil, where he is petitioned in particularly urgent cases. Expeditus is invoked for the speedy resolution of personal problems, lawsuits, and business matters. He is a favorite of procrastinators, jobseekers, and of those conducting business on the web, where he is noted as the unofficial patron of hackers. A *Facebook* page is maintained in his name.

The site *saintexpedite.org* describes the proper way to request help of St. Expeditus.

> Don't ask any evil favors.
> Ask one favor at a time.
> Ask politely.
> Ask from the heart.
> Light a red candle or for financial matters, a green one.
> Wednesdays are the best days for petitions, as this was also the day of Mercury, the Roman god with wings on his heels.
> If you make a promise to him, carry through.
> If he answers your prayer, pay him, for he was a soldier paid for his service.

What payment does St. Expeditus appreciate most? Fresh flowers—not plastic or silk ones—and poundcake. Sarah Lee will do.

Joseph

(1st century)
March 19

Fathers, Families, Carpenters, Cabinetmakers, Craftspeople, Real estate, Engineers,
Working people, Confectioners, Doubt, The dying, For a good death

Descendant of David, carpenter and builder, husband of Mary: Joseph was the father Jesus needed to protect and guide him on earth.

The medieval *Golden Legend* includes the betrothal story of Joseph found in Eastern Orthodox tradition—that a husband was to be chosen for Mary, and the temple priests had all unmarried men of the house of David bring a branch to the altar. The priests followed Isaiah's prophecy: they would give Mary into the care of the man whose branch flowered and onto which a dove of the Holy Ghost came to rest.

One by one, the unmarried men laid their branches on the altar, and there they remained, plain wood branches. Joseph hung back, for being an older widower with children, he believed himself unsuitable as husband to such a young girl. The priests called him forward, however, and when Joseph laid his branch on the altar, it burst into blossom and a dove flew down to it.

The Gospel of Matthew tells that Joseph and Mary were betrothed, but before the marriage, it was discovered that she was with child. "A just man," Joseph could not bear to abandon her to the danger of a public shaming; he thought perhaps to send her away quietly to some private place.

In the midst of his painful deliberations, an angel visited him in a dream and told him that the child Mary carried was the Lord's. His name would be Jesus, and he was destined to save humanity from its sins. Joseph's dilemma fell away; he heeded the angel and married Mary, thus giving her his protection.

Jesus was born in Bethlehem in Judea, a land King Herod ruled. Men who had journeyed from the East sought an audience with the king to ask him, "Where is this new King of the Jews, who has just been born?" They had ridden toward a strange star to find the child so that they could worship him with gifts they had brought. Disturbed, Herod called his priests and scribes and commanded them to reveal where this child was.

"Bethlehem," they said, "for that is what the prophet wrote."

Herod secretly summoned the men from the East. He told them to search out the child and to inform him of its whereabouts so that he, too, could worship. The men traveled with the star until it stood still, and then finding the child, they bowed with joy and laid out precious things from the East: gold, frankincense with its fragrance of lemon and pine, and dark, earthy myrrh. They departed by another route for their own country because God warned them in a dream not to return to King Herod.

An angel appeared in Joseph's dreams, saying to take Mary and Jesus away from Herod into Egypt and to wait there. This Joseph did.

Herod was wild with fury that the men from the East had evaded him. How would he destroy this King of the Jews, who threatened his own power? He ordered all male infants in Bethlehem, two years old and younger, murdered. His soldiers carried out his bloody decree, and wails tore the air of Bethlehem.

Joseph guarded his family in Egypt until the angel reentered his dreams, saying Herod was dead, and the family could make their way back to Israel. But

Joseph was wary of the present king, the slaughterer Herod's son, and he took Mary and Jesus into Galilee and settled them in the city of Nazareth.

The Gospel of Luke tells Mary's story, and one from Jesus's childhood. The family went every year to Jerusalem for the feast of the Passover. When Jesus was twelve, they went as they always had done, and when they left, Jesus stayed behind without their knowing. They traveled a distance believing the boy together with the whole company but finding he was not, Joseph and Mary turned straightaway and went back to Jerusalem.

They searched for three days among their kin and acquaintances. Finally they discovered Jesus in the temple, sitting among the learned, listening, questioning, and astonishing these teachers with the depth of his understanding. The sight confused his parents. Mary appealed to him, "Son, why have you treated us like this? Your father and I looked for you in many places."

Neither she nor Joseph understood the boy's answer: "Why did you look for me? Did you not know that I must be about my Father's business?" Jesus went with them back to Nazareth then and was obedient to them.

There the Bible leaves Joseph. He must have been dead by the time of the crucifixion, as Jesus entrusted his mother's care to his beloved disciple John.

But early Christians did not want to leave Joseph; they wanted to know more about him, to remember him. Perhaps they wanted this just man rewarded, watched over by a powerful son as they yearned to be watched over on their last day.

Among the apocrypha is a manuscript titled *The History of Joseph the Carpenter*, which contains a detailed chronicle of Joseph's death, purportedly narrated by Jesus to his disciples. This manuscript tells that after Joseph settled his family in Nazareth, he went back "to his trade of a carpenter, earned his living by the work of his hands; for … he never sought to live for nothing by another's hands." His present age is given as 111 years; nevertheless he mourned the loss of his precious life as every human does, "for great fear and intense sadness take hold of all bodies on the day of their death."

Joseph's children and Mary and his stepson Jesus were gathered around his bed. Jesus saw Death coming with its army of flames and saw the tears in Joseph's eyes and heard his anguished sighs. He drove back Death's army and asked God to send:

> Michael, prince of Thine angels, and Gabriel, the herald of light, and all the light of Thine angels and let the whole of their array walk with the soul of my father Joseph until they have conducted it to Thee. … And Michael and Gabriel came to the soul of my father Joseph, and took it, and wrapped it in a shining wrapper.

Jesus embraced Joseph's body and wept over it. Then the men of Nazareth laid this good old father in the tomb beside the body of his own father.

94

Lucy

(283-304)
December 13

Light, Perception, Eyesight, Eye trouble, Forms of blindness,
Opticians, Ophthalmologists

"'Tis the year's midnight, and it is the day's, Lucy's, who scarce seven hours herself unmasks," wrote John Donne. After St. Lucy's night, the light stays with us longer each day, until it wakes spring's buds and at last shines wide on the grasses of summer.

> Enjoy your summer all,
> Since she enjoys her long night's festival.
> Let me prepare towards her, and let me call
> This hour her vigil, and her eve, since this
> Both the year's and the day's deep midnight is.

Lucy, meaning "light," was a girl with light's qualities: beauty, grace, cleanliness, and straightness of purpose. Born in Syracusa, she was of noble family, betrothed to a nobleman. One story tells that this suitor could not stop praising the sparkle of her eyes. Lucy, fearing such extravagant admiration was a flowery path to hell, removed her eyes with a knife and sent them to the young man on a plate. Her remorseful betrothed became a Christian, and as the blinded Lucy knelt in prayer, God restored both her sight and her shining eyes.

The Golden Legend tells a different tale: Lucy's mother Eutychia fell ill with a hemorrhage, and in four years, no one could cure it. The young woman took her mother to St. Agatha's tomb in Catania; they arrived during a mass just as the priest read a passage about a similar healing. Lucy urged her mother to believe in the saint's power to heal and believing, to touch Agatha's tomb. The sick woman and her daughter lingered to pray after everyone else had gone. In the twilit place Lucy fell asleep.

She dreamed of a wreath of angels, in their midst St. Agatha, who chided her: Why had Lucy asked the saint for something she herself could do? See—her faith had already cured her mother.

Lucy woke and found it to be true: Eutychia was healed. Lucy begged then to be released from a promise of marriage and to give to the poor the money and goods that were her dowry.

"Wait until you've closed my eyes," Eutychia said, "then give away our wealth."

"But we leave our fortune in death because we cannot take it with us. Now while we are alive, we should give, for that giving is worthy of reward."

They went home and began to distribute their possessions. Hearing of this, Lucy's betrothed asked her old nurse why the poor were now carrying away precious things he would claim by marriage. The nurse blurted out that Lucy had found a better property for him and was selling off her goods to buy it. So the young man helped them, but discovering the truth later, he angrily denounced Lucy as a Christian to the Roman consul Paschasius, and condemned her for acting against Caesar's law.

Paschasius had Lucy brought before the dais where he sat in his consul's chair. Glaring down at her, he ordered, "Offer a sacrifice to the gods."

"God loves those sacrifices we make for the poor," said the girl, "and since I have given away all I own, I offer to Him myself."

"Tell that story to fools," said Paschasius. "Not to me, for I live by the laws of my masters."

"You live by Caesar's laws, I live by God's. You want to please your masters, I want to please the Lord. Do with me whatever you must, and I will do what I know is right."

"You have wasted your father's fortune!"

"I have put my fortune in a safe place."

Paschasius vowed that the whip would silence her and called his torturer.

"The words of God," said the girl, "cannot be stilled."

The consul thrust forward, pointing his gold-ringed finger. "So *you* are God?"

"I am the handmaid of God, and the holy spirit speaks from my mouth."

"The holy spirit is in *you*?"

"All who lead chaste lives are temples of the holy spirit," Lucy said.

Smiling, the consul settled back into his chair. "Take this girl to a brothel. Her body will be defiled there and the holy spirit driven out."

"Unless the mind consents," Lucy answered, "the body is never defiled. Do you believe you can reach my will or my soul, you son of the devil?"

Paschasius ordered that a crowd be gathered and instructed to abuse the girl until they had killed her. He signaled minions to carry her out to the rowdy crowd. These men seized Lucy's thin arms, her shoulders, her waist, but it seemed they had taken hold of iron, for they could not lift the girl.

Paschasius then called a thousand men, and he had Lucy's hands and feet bound, but these thousand could not move her.

The consul commanded that a thousand yoke of oxen be herded in and fastened to her, and the oxen could not drag her away.

Court magicians were summoned, but their spells proved useless and their wands waved like children's toys.

The frantic consul resorted to a tactic against what he believed to be Lucy's sorcery: he had urine thrown over her, and when still she stood unmoved, he caused a bonfire to be built around her and boiling oil poured over her head.

"All this you do," said Lucy, "will free unbelievers from the fear of suffering."

A friend of the consul's ran forward and buried his dagger in the girl's throat. But Lucy spoke all the same, a prophecy: the persecutors would tumble from their seats of power. As Agatha had been given to Catania as protector, so she would be given to Syracusa.

As she finished speaking, the harsh tramp of soldiers was heard. Centurions marched into the hall, chained Paschasius, and led him off to Rome to answer for his looting of the province.

Lucy still held her bit of ground. She did not die until a Christian priest fed her the Body of the Lord, until the people in the hall echoed her own last word, Amen.

> At the next world, that is, at the next spring,
> I am every dead thing
> In whom Love wrought new alchemy.
> —John Donne, "A Nocturnal upon St. Lucy's Day"

Sources

I referred to Butler's *Lives of the Saints*, Jacobus de Voragine's *The Golden Legend*, the King James and Revised Standard editions of the Bible, and Wikipedia for information on the saints' lives, in addition to the specific sources listed below, and to the files that Catherine Ferguson has maintained for forty years. These files, used to compose the saints' stories that Ms. Ferguson writes on the back of her retablos, contain hundreds of old copied pages—their edges snipped, as Catherine is a great one for scissors—so that not all sources could be fully identified.

Agatha

Alford, Violet. "The Cat Saint." *Folklore* 52, no. 3 (1941): 161-183.

De Voragine, Jacobus. *The Golden Legend: Readings on the Saints,* Vol. 1, 154-57. Translated by William Granger Ryan. Princeton: Princeton University Press, 1993.

García Lorca, Federico. "The Martydom of St. Eulalia" In *The Selected Poems of Federico Garcia Lorca,* edited by Francisco García Lorca and Donald Merriam Allen. New York: New Directions Publishing Corporation, 2005.

Anne

Walker, Alexander, trans. "Protoevangelium of James." In *The Ante-Nicene Fathers,* Vol. 8, edited by Alexander Roberts, James Donaldson, and A. Cleveland Cox. Buffalo, NY: Christian Literature Publishing Co., 1886.

Anthony of Padua

Dal-Gal, Niccolo. "St. Anthony of Padua." In *The Catholic Encyclopedia,* Vol. 1. New York: Robert Appleton Co., 1907. http://www.newadvent.org/cathen/01556a.htm.

Online Encyclopedia. "Franciscans." *Online Encyclopedia.* http://encyclopedia.jrank.org/FRA_GAE/FRANCISCANS_otherwise_called_Fr.html.

Kosmicki, Greg. "The Patron Saint of Lost and Found." In *The Patron Saint of Lost and Found.* Omaha: Lone Willow Press, 2003.

Watson, Brandon. "Anthony and the Fishes." *Siris.* http://www.branemrys.blogspot.com/2006/06/anthony-and-fishes.html.

Brendan

All Saints Parish. "Commemoration of St. Brendan of Ardfert and Clonert." *All Saints Parish Celtic Spirituality.* http://www.allsaintsbrookline.org/celtic_saints/brendan.html.

Lawless, Emily. "Fontenoy 1745." *Poetry X Archive.* http://poetry.poetryx.com/poems/11119/.

Ó Donnchadha, Gearóid. *St. Brendan of Kerry, the Navigator.* Dublin: Open Air, 2004.

Brigid

Butler, Alban. *Lives of the Saints,* 20. Files of Catherine Ferguson.

Lady Gregory. *A Book of Saints and Wonders,* 15-22. New York: Oxford Press, 1971.

Reilly, Robert. *Irish Saints,* 16-26. New York: Vision Books, 1964.

Saiser, Marge. *St. Bridgit Speaks.* As yet unpublished.

Catherine of Alexandria:

De Voragine, Jacobus. *The Golden Legend: Readings on the Saints,* Vol. 2, 334-41. Translated by William Granger Ryan. Princeton: Princeton University Press, 1993.

Gamma Kappa Pi. "St. Catherine of Alexandria—A Story for Our Time." *Gamma Kappa Phi.* http://www.kappagammapi.org/_catherine.html.

Vann, Joseph. "Saint Catherine of Alexandria, Virgin, martyr." In *Lives of Saints.* John J. Crawley & Co., Inc., 1954. http://www.ewtn.com/library/mary/catherin.htm.

Christopher

De Voragine, Jacobus. *The Golden Legend: Readings on the Saints*, Vol. 2, 10-14. Translated by William Granger Ryan. Princeton: Princeton University Press, 1993.

Dymphna

Jones, Terry H. "Saint Dymphna." *Saints.SQPM.com.* http://saints.sqpn.com/saint-dymphna/.

Kirsch, Johann Peter. "St. Dymphna." In *The Catholic Encyclopedia*, Vol. 5. New York: Robert Appleton Co., 1909. http://www.newadvent.org/cathen/05221b.htm.

Wikipedia. "Dymphna" *Wikipedia.* http://en.wikipedia.org/wiki/Dymphna.

Expeditus

Expedite "History of Saint Expedite.org." *Saint Expedite.org.* http://saintexpedite.org/history.html.

Facebook. "St. Expeditus." *Facebook.* http://www.facebook.com/pages/St-Expeditus/102910666416652.

Votum Solvit Libens Merito. "Glossary of Roman Military Terms." *Votum Solvit Libens Merito.* http://votumsolvit.com/2010/05/16/glossary-of-roman-military-terms/.

Wikipedia. "St. Expeditus." *Wikipedia.* http://en.wikipedia.org/wiki/St_Expeditus.

Francis of Assisi

Cunningham, Lawrence, ed. *Brother Francis.* New York: Harper & Row, 1972.

De Voragine, Jacobus. *The Golden Legend: Readings on the Saints,* Vol. 2, 220-30. Translated by William Granger Ryan. Princeton: Princeton University Press, 1993.

Habig, Marion Alphonse, ed. "St. Francis of Assisi: Writings and Early Biographies." Chicago: Franciscan Herald Press, 1973.

Kazantzakis, Nikos. *Saint Francis of Assisi.* New York: Simon & Schuster, 1962.

Robinson, Paschal. "St. Francis of Assisi." In *The Catholic Encyclopedia,* Vol. 6. New York: Robert Appleton Co., 1909. http://www.newadvent.org/cathen/06221a.htm.

Gabriel

"Book of Daniel," 10: 5-21. *Holy Bible.*

"The Gospel According to St. Luke," 1:10-20, 1:26-37. *Holy Bible.*

Guadalupe

Brading, D.A. *Mexican Phoenix.* Cambridge University Press, 2001.

Poole, Stafford. *Our Lady of Guadalupe: The Origins and Sources of a Mexican National Symbol.* Tucson: University of Arizona Press, 1966.

Zarebska, Carla. *Guadalupe.* Translated by Jacqueline Robinson Lopez. Photographs by Alejandro Gomez de Tuddo. Oaxaca, Mexico: Equipar S. A. de C. V, 2002.

Guererro Rosado, Jose Luis, trans. "Nican mopohua (Here is recounted)" In *Guadalupe*, by Carla Zarebska. Mexico: Equipar S. A. de C. V, 2002.

James

Camerlynck, Achille. "St. James the Greater." In *The Catholic Encyclopedia*, Vol. 8. New York: Robert Appleton Co., 1910. http://www.newadvent.org/cathen/08279b.htm.

Catholic-saints.net. "St. James the Greater." *Catholic Saints*. http://www.catholic-saints.net/saints/st-james.php.

De Voragine, Jacobus. *The Golden Legend: Readings on the Saints*, Vol. 2, 3-10. Translated by William Granger Ryan. Princeton: Princeton University Press, 1993.

Simmons, Mark, Donna Pierce, and Joan Myers. *Santiago: Saint of Two Worlds*. Albuquerque: The University of New Mexico Press, 1991.

"The Acts of the Apostles," 12:2. *Holy Bible*.

"The Gospel According to St. Mark," 3:17. 10:35-41. *Holy Bible*.

"The Gospel According to St. Matthew," 20:20-24. *Holy Bible*.

Saint James Episcopal Church of Las Cruces, New Mexico. "Who Was St. James the Greater?" *St. James Episcopal Church*. http://www.saintjameslc.com/stjames.html.

Jerome

Butler, Alban. *Lives of the Saints*, 307-10. Edited by Michael Walsh. HarperSanFrancisco, 1991.

De Voragine, Jacobus. *The Golden Legend: Readings on the Saints*, Vol. 2, 211-16. Translated by William Granger Ryan. Princeton: Princeton University Press, 1993.

Wright, F.A., trans. *Select Letters of St. Jerome*. Edited by G.P. Goold. Cambridge: Harvard University Press, 1980.

Joan of Arc

Gies, Frances. *Joan of Arc, the Legend and the Reality*. New York: Harper & Row, 1981.

Pernoud, Regine. *Joan of Arc by Herself and her Witnesses*. Translated by Edward Hyams. London: Macdonald & Co., Ltd., 1964.

—— and Marie Veronique Clin. *Joan of Arc: Her Story*. Translated by Jeremy duQuesney Adams. New York: St. Martin's Press, 1998.

John of the Cross

McKennitt, Loreena. "Dark Night of the Soul." *Jos Van Geffen*. http://www.xs4all.nl/~josvg/cits/lm/lorecd53.html.

Merton, Thomas. "St. John of the Cross." *Catholic Information Network*. http://www.cin.org/saints/jcross-merton.html.

St. John of the Cross. *Dark Night of the Soul*. Translated by Mirabai Starr. New York: Riverhead, 2002.

Zimmerman, Benedict. "St. John of the Cross." In *The Catholic Encyclopedia*, Vol. 8. New York: Robert Appleton Co., 1910. http://www.newadvent.org/cathen/08480a.htm.

Joseph

Roberts, Alexander and James Donaldson, eds. "The History of Joseph the Carpenter." In *The Ante-Nicene Fathers: Translations of the Writings of the Fathers Down to a.d. 325*,

Vol. 8. Grand Rapids: William B. Eerdmans Publishing Co., 1951.

"The Gospel According to St. Luke," 1:27-80, 2:1-52. *Holy Bible.*

"The Gospel According to St. Matthew," 1:1-25, 2: 1-23. *Holy Bible.*

Librada

"Librada." Files of Catherine Ferguson.

Note at Santuario de Chimayó, summer 1995.

Lucy

Bridge, James. "St. Lucy." In *The Catholic Enclyclopedia*, Vol. 9. New York: Robert Appleton Co., 1910. http://www.newadvent.org/cathen/09414a.htm.

De Voragine, Jacobus. *The Golden Legend: Readings on the Saints,* Vol. 1, 27-29. Translated by William Granger Ryan. Princeton: Princeton University Press, 1993.

Donne, John. "A Nocturnal Upon St. Lucy's Day, Being the Shortest Day." In *The Complete and Selected Prose of John Donne.* Edited by Charles M. Coffin. New York: The Modern Library, 1994.

Luke

Aherne, Cornelius. "Gospel of St. Luke." *The Catholic Encyclopedia*, Vol. 9. New York: Robert Appleton Co., 1910. http://www.newadvent.org/cathen/09420a.htm.

De Voragine, Jacobus. *The Golden Legend: Readings on the Saints,* Vol. 2, 247-54. Translated by William Granger Ryan. Princeton: Princeton University Press, 1993.

"The Gospel According to St. Luke." *Holy Bible.*

"The Acts of the Apostles." *Holy Bible.*

"The Second Epistle of Paul the Apostle to Timothy," 4:6-11. *Holy Bible.*

Wikipedia. "Gospel of Luke." *Wikipedia.* http://en.wikipedia.org/wiki/Gospel_of_luke.

María de Ágreda:

Colahan, Clark. *The Visions of Sor María de Ágreda.* Tucson: The University of Arizona Press, 1994.

De Benavides, Fray Alonso. *The Memorial of 1630.* Translated by Mrs. Edward E. Ayer. Albuquerque: Horn and Wallace, Publishers, 1965.

Fedewa, Marilyn H. "Jumano Native Americans Still Revere Lady in Blue." In *Tradición* 13, no. 2. (2008): 18-20.

Martha

De Voragine, Jacobus. *The Golden Legend: Readings on the Saints,* Vol. 2, 23-26. Translated by William Granger Ryan. Princeton: Princeton University Press, 1993.

"The Gospel According to St. John," 11:1-44, 12:2. *Holy Bible.*

"The Gospel According to St. Luke," 10:38-42. *Holy Bible.*

Martin de Porres

Cavallini, Giulianna. *St. Martin de Porres, Apostle of Charity.* Translated by Caroline Holland. St. Louis: B. Herder Book Co., 1963.

——. *I Fioretti del Beato Martino.* Translated by Caroline Holland. Rome: Edizione Cateriniane, 1957.

De Voragine, Jacobus. *The Golden Legend: Readings on the Saints,* Vol. 1, 374-83. Translated by William Granger Ryan. Princeton: Princeton University Press, 1993.

Garcia-Rivera, Alex. "St. Martin de Porres: The 'Little Stories' and the Semiotics of Culture." Marynoll, New York: Orbis Books, 1995.

Mary Magdalene

Kassia. (Kassiane, Icasia). Hymn: "Troparion" or "Mary Magdalene." Translated by Liana Sakelliou. Second translation by AB, WB, and Elena Kolb. Files of Catherine Ferguson.

Robinson, J.M., ed. "The Gospel of Philip," 145, 148. "The Dialogue of the Savior," 252-253. "The Gospel of Mary," 526-527. In *Nag Hammadi Library*. Translated by Members of the Coptic Gnostic Library Project. Rev., E.J. Brill. HarperSanFrancisco, 1990.

Pearse, Roger. "The Nag Hammadi Discovery of Manuscripts." *Roger Pearse's Pages*. http://www.tertullian.org/rpearse/manuscripts/nag_hammadi.htm.

Schaberg, Jane. *The Resurrection of Mary Magdalene*. New York: Continuum, 2002.

Schmidt, Carl and Violet MacDermott, trans. "Pistis Sophia: Book One." *Pseudepigrapha, Apocrypha and Sacred Writings.* http://www.pseudepigrapha.com/PistisSophia/pistisSophia_Book1.html.

"The Gospel According to Matthew," 28:1-10. *Holy Bible.*

"The Gospel According to Mark," 14:1-9, 16:7-9. *Holy Bible.*

"The Gospel According to Luke," 8:2, 7:36-42, 24:1. *Holy Bible.*

"The Gospel According to John," 20:14-18. *Holy Bible.*

"The Proverbs," 31:25-26, 31. *Holy Bible.*

Matthew

De Voragine, Jacobus. *The Golden Legend: Readings on the Saints*, Vol. 2, 183-88. Translated by William Granger Ryan. Princeton: Princeton University Press, 1993.

"The Gospel According to St. Luke," 5:27-32. *Holy Bible.*

"The Gospel According to St. Mark," 2:14-17. *Holy Bible.*

"The Gospel According to St. Matthew," 9:9-11. *Holy Bible.*

Michael

"Book of Daniel," 12:1. *Holy Bible.*

Free Republic "Apparition of St. Michael the Archangel." *Free Republic.* http://www.freerepublic.com/focus/news/2246754/posts.

Holweck, Frederick. "St. Michael the Archangel." In *The Catholic Encyclopedia*, Vol. 10. New York: Robert Appleton Company, 1911. http://www.newadvent.org/cathen/10275b.htm.

Paratrooper Prayers. "St. Michael the archangel, Patron Saint of the Airborne." *Paratrooper Prayers.* http://paratrooperprayers.tripod.com/id12.html.

"Revelation," 12:7-9. *Holy Bible.*

Vann, Joseph. "St. Michael—Archangel.." In *Lives of Saints.* John J. Crawley & Co., Inc., 1954. http://www.ewtn.com/library/MARY/MICHAEL.HTM.

Wikipedia. "Michael (archangel)." *Wikipedia.* http://en.wikipedia.org/wiki/Michael_%28archangel%29.

Pascual

DePalma, Gina. "Zabaione." *Babbo Ristorante e Enoteca.* http://www.babbonyc.com/dolci-zabaione.html.

Giffords, Gloria Fraser. "Saints as Subjects." In *Mexican Folk Retablos*. Albuquerque: University of New Mexico Press, 1992.

Palmer, Gabrielle. "The Reluctant Saint." Files of Catherine Ferguson.
Stanisforth, Oswald. "St. Pascal Baylon." In *The Catholic Encyclopedia*, Vol. 11. New York: Robert Appleton Company, 1911. http://www.newadvent.org/cathen/11512a.htm.

Raphael
Charles, R.H., trans. "Book of Enoch, 1917." *Sacred Texts.* http://www.sacred-texts.com/bib/boe/.
Driscoll, James F. "St. Raphael." In *The Catholic Encyclopedia*, Vol. 12. New York: Robert Appleton Co., 1911. http://www.newadvent.org/cathen/12640b.htm.
New World Encyclopedia. "Raphael (Archangel)." *New World Encyclopedia.* http://www.newworldencyclopedia.org/entry/Raphael_%28Archangel%29.
"Tobit," Chapters 1-14. *Holy Bible* King James version (Apocrypha). http://etext.virginia.edu/toc/modeng/public/KjvTobi.html.

Rosa de Lima
Capes, F.M. *The Flowers of the New World.* London: R. & T. Washbourne, 1899.
De Bussierre, quoted In *The Flowers of the New World,* 113-14, by F.M. Capes. London: R. & T. Washbourne, 1899.
Vann, Joseph. "Saint Rose of Lima." In *Lives of Saints.* John J. Crawley & Co., Inc., 1954. http://www.ewtn.com/library/MARY/ROSE.HTM.

Teresa de Ávila
Gross, Francis, Jr. and Toni Perrier Gross. *The Making of a Mystic.* Albany: State University of New York Press, 1993.
Newland, Mary Reed. *The Saint Book.* Files of Catherine Ferguson.
Matz, Terry. "St. Teresa de Ávila—Doctor of the Church." *Catholic Online.* http://www.catholic.org/saints/saint.php?saint_id=208.
Teresa de Ávila. *Interior Castles.* Translated by E. Allison Peers. New York: Image Books Doubleday, 1961.
——"In the Hands of God." *Poetry Chaikhana.* http://www.poetry-chaikhana.com/T/TeresaofAvil/InHsofGod.htm.
——"The Life of Teresa de Jesus." Translated and Edited by E. Allison Peers. New York: Image Books Doubleday, 1960.
"Teresa of Ávila." *Poet Seers.* http://www.poetseers.org/spiritual_and_devotional_poets/christian/teresa_of_avila/.

Valentine
Chaucer, Geoffrey. "The Parliament of Fowls." In *The Riverside Chaucer, 3rd Edition.* Houghton Mifflin, 1987.
Michalove, Sharon. "The Great Marriage Hunt: Finding a Wife in Fifteenth Century England." *EServer.* http://history.eserver.org/finding-a-wife.txt.
Paston Family. *Paston letters and Papers of the 15th Century.* Edited by Norman Davis. Oxford: Clarendon Press, 1953. http://ota.oucs.ox.ac.uk/headers/1685.xml.
Wikipedia. "Saint Valentine." *Wikipedia.* http://en.wikipedia.org/wiki/Saint_Valentine.
Thurston, Herbert. "St. Valentine." *The Catholic Encyclopedia*, Vol 15. New York: Robert Appleton Co., 1912. http://www.newadvent.org/cathen/15254a.htm.

9034230R0

Made in the USA
Charleston, SC
04 August 2011